DATE DUE

JUL 0 6 1993	NOV 0 9 2002	
NOV 2 4 1993	SEP 2 1 2004	
JAN 1 9 1994		
APR 2 9 1994		
FEB 2 7 1995		
APR 1 1 1995		
OCT 1 1 1995		
DEC 0 5 1996		
FEB 7 1998		
FEB 2 4 2000		
MAR 1 4 2001		
APR 0 4 2002		
MAY 2 8 2002		
JUN 2 0 2002		
JUL 0 5 2002		
OCT 0 8 2002		
JAN 2 5 2003		

american INDIAN POTTERY

AN IDENTIFICATION AND VALUE GUIDE

by
JOHN W. BARRY

BOOKS AMERICANA
INC

P.O. BOX 2326 • FLORENCE, ALABAMA • 35630

PHOTO CREDITS

*Listed Alphabetically by
Photographer and Figure Number.*

Leslie Allison   130, 288, 381, 523, 524, 527, 626, 627.

John Barry   7, 171, 172, 266, 304, 321, 323, 324, 331-333, 369, 370, 385, 389, 403, 404, 416, 417, 423, 424, 461, 579.

Mike Boyatt   60-68.

Bill Ciesla   120-124, 243, 250, 275, 293 300, 301, 307, 308, 310, 312, 320, 322, 326, 327, 330, 337, 339, 391, 458, 495, 506, 526, 596-602.

H. T. Cory   412.

Edward S. Curtis   637.

William S. Fowler   32-35, 37.

John Garcia   429, 443-448.

Vic Hogsett   125.

David Ichelson   449, 595, 643, 654, 655

Henry Johnson   126.

R. Keck   233, 413, 418-421, 568.

Marguerite Kernaghan   109-111, 113, 157, 158, 182, 186, 187, 190, 496, 497, 536, 635.

Stewart Kernaghan   108, 112, 114-117, 119, 139, 159, 160, 178, 188, 189, 192, 193, 207, 245, 270, 383, 594.

Bill Klein   311, 329, 341, 362-364, 409, 466, 480, 490, 492, 502-504, 514.

Fred E. Mang, Jr.   (page 47), 87-90.

E. H. Maude   216.

Barry Powell   586.

Peter Pilles   A-F

William L. Rada   131, 177, 232, 264, 285, 286, 287A, 287B, 299, 414, 415, 525.

Revised Edition

ISBN 0-89689-047-3

2   3   4   5   6   7   8   9   0   -   85   84

CONTENTS

FOREWORD

Few people have had deeper or wider contact with things Indian than the author of this book. As a child, John W. "Jack" Barry absorbed local prehistory in Virginia. During vacation travels he became familiar with the crafts and cultures of the Great Smoky Mountain Cherokee and Florida Seminole Indians. The traces of early peoples were examined in Ohio's Miami Valley, with monumental remains of Hopewell earthworks and random finds of still older projectile points.

Jack also visited the North Central States in search of knowledge concerning the Indian eras. Before graduating from the University of Cincinnati, he served as a seasonal Park Ranger at Yellowstone National Park.

There he became interested in the Bannock and Sheepeater Indians of the Yellowstone Plateau. Jack also explored Utah's Salt Lake Desert and observed evidence of the Fremont and Anasazi culture's influence in the Great Basin.

While living in Utah, he investigated prehistoric pottery and the long-ago peoples who had made them. Deciding to approach the past by a focus on the present, he began to study the potters along the Rio Grande River in New Mexico.

"Then", Jack recounts, "I became so interested in present day Pueblos—and the Pueblo people, their contemporary pottery where I discovered clues to understanding prehistoric people and their pottery—that I did not go back to the prehistoric". Living the past few years in Davis, California, Jack is involved in the world of Native American ceramics. It is something he understands well.

In addition to contacts with other experts in the field, Jack does intensive research on Indian pottery and the Pueblo Cultures. The outstanding library at the University of California, Davis, Campus, is conveniently located for his research. His vacations from his scientific profession are spent visiting early sites and he is familiar with many of the major Southwestern museums, especially the pottery departments.

Seeking to know Indian pottery by meeting those who create it, Jack regularly visits Southwestern ceramic makers. He asks questions, makes observations, and takes notes. Jack has learned the practical and esoteric details that mean the difference between a good piece and a fine piece. He has special relationships with a number of potters, which give him a unique position from which to comment on this art form.

A communicator of rank, Jack has written articles on Indian pottery for various newspapers, plus the pottery section of the book, *North American Indian Artifacts*. He has been profiled in *The Indian Trader*, a respected publication on American Indians and their arts and is listed in *Who's Who in the West*.

Beyond all this, the educational aspect of Indian pottery concerns Jack to the extent that he has given talks and demonstrations on pottery making. He frequently visits shows and shops to talk with prospective buyers about pottery styles and techniques. In short, Jack is involved in many phases of this field, from pre-manufacture, to education.

Knowing Jack, and his thorough comprehension of this area, one trait has always impressed me. It is his willingness to inform. Many people with accumulated facts tend to hoard them for some unknown personal satisfaction. Fortunately, Jack Barry thrives by sharing, by dispensing accurate information, as this book attests.

Much writing on this subject—and no major book of this type has appeared for a number of years—tends to be either so highly technical that few can benefit or so general that any real contribution is lacking.

This publication strikes a reasonable balance. The coverage is comprehensive, including the significant pottery regions of this country. Values aid in judging artistic worth for the contemporary wares.

Timespans are covered in detail, prehistoric, historic and comtemporary. The writing is easily understood, the style crisp and direct, the photographs excellent. The whole provides an overview of American Indian pottery that will not be found elsewhere.

This important book is the culmination of many years of purposeful and enjoyable research. And it could only have been written by Jack Barry, a man who knows, loves, and respects his subject, and the potters, past and present. The book is an intelligent summing up of a multifaceted and key part of the American Indian lifeway.

Lar Hothem
Carrol, Ohio
May 1980

PREFACE

American Indian pottery is enjoying a period of heightened activity as both Indian and non-Indian share in the excitement of a rediscovery. Somehow I fell victim to this excitement and began to ask questions about a seemingly straight forward craft. As the information began to stack up and be sorted it soon became apparent that these clay figurines, canteens, urns, and bowls were an artistic representation of native peoples past and present, symbolizing a relationship to the earth, to the sky, and beyond. While sharing the pottery experience with a modern Pueblo, one can feel her sensitivity and deep concern for this art form. The enthusiasm and pride of a modern day Indian potter as she describes and demonstrates the techniques of making pottery reflects a long tradition of her people. Fortunate are those with whom they are willing to share this enthusiasm as their pottery takes on a reflection of the past and the present. One can drift back with time to the ancient cliff dwellers inhabiting the declivitous slopes and precipitous ledges of the Southwest and imagine the potter's difficult role. She had to perform the daily domestic chores which often meant the difference between death and survival, but also had to create culturally acceptable pottery.

It is not by coincidence that the story of North American Indian pottery has its focal point in the Southwest. Here, pottery reached a high form of development, and unlike the central and eastern United States, the Southwest has had an uninterrupted history of pottery production, continuing to the present. Pottery developed as an essential to life from utilitarian, commercial, social, and ceremonial viewpoints. Evidence of its use is found in abundance throughout the Southwest, wherever agricultural cultures inhabited the desert and mesas. An understanding of Indian pottery is basic to the study of the pottery-producing cultures and their peoples. There is no other art form which reveals such an abundance of information about these cultures. Perhaps this is our motivation in pursuing knowledge of ceramic art of the prehistoric, historic, and modern ceramist. To hold and examine a fine pot is to share an experience with the potter.

Pottery of the Southwest has been described by numerous authors and students representing archaeologists, anthropologists, collectors, artists, and others who have been motivated to understand the origin and development of this ceramic art form. With this in mind, an attempt has been made to present only an overview of North

7

American Indian pottery, and to document values of contemporary pottery at a point in time. Except for continuity in presenting the sequence of pottery, I have attempted to avoid repeating what these outstanding authors have presented so capably. The task has been difficult because of the discovery that, while source material is abundant for Southwestern pottery, there is a void of appropriate reference for pottery from other areas of North America. Additionally, without travel to each location, it is nearly impossible to ascertain the current level and scope of ceramic activities. As a result, this book does not treat all pottery types equitably. Due to administrative and some logistical restraints, there are obvious omissions.

There is no suggestion through omission that certain groups, past or present, did not contribute measureably to this ceramic history of North America.

Present day production and trading of Indian pottery is based primarily in the Southwest, but there has been a slight revival of the pottery tradition in the Southeast. Also, non-traditional types are being produced by other Native American groups who have no prior pottery tradition in their history. These are omitted from the discussion as the book addresses pottery produced by groups which historically have a pottery tradition.

Frequently, I am asked to suggest a reference on Indian pottery. Which of the numerous books would best serve the person who has an initial curiosity? Where has the entire subject been surveyed in a manner which is not too technical, but complete enough to satisfy the beginning student? Can the subject be treated in one volume and still result in a meaningful contribution? It is with this thought in mind that I have attempted to present an overview to be used as a reference by those persons who have initial interest in contemporary North American Indian pottery.

The book also was initiated in response to a need for a reference of trade values. Values have been assigned as a guide to some historic and to modern pottery produced after 1900. Values vary widely for many reasons, and therefore, should be used only as a guide to some historic and to modern pottery produced after 1900. No attempt has been made to assign values to prehistoric pottery, to pottery in public and private institutional collections, or to certain pieces in private collections. Values assigned to each item are the sole responsibility of the author. The subject of values will be discussed in more detail within the text.

Specific references to individual potters and others associated with pottery are for reference and illustrative purposes. There is no conscious suggestion made to judge potters relative to others; however, several are listed who have achieved national fame for their ceramic achievements.

There are hundreds of potters, both past and present, who have made significant contributions to sustaining and developing the art of pottery during historic times. There are a few hundred students, collectors, archaeologists, and traders who have played major roles in timely efforts which have encouraged and sustained the art. For those who are interested in further research into the development of pottery and the personalities associated with it, a list of references is provided in the Appendix under Sources and Selected References.

ACKNOWLEDGEMENTS

The success of this project was dependent upon the assistance and generous contributions of numerous persons and institutions who provided information and photographs; and who shared their knowledge and interest in native ceramic art. Contributions from a broad public and private sector were essential to developing a reference of such a broad coverage.

Lar Hothem, known writer on North American Indians, suggested that this book be written. He provided encouragement, suggestions, and sources of information for which I express my deepest appreciation.

I am particularly indebted to my wife, Patricia, for editing and typing; to Jean Oliver for typing the countless letters; and to Janet Zacharias for her patience and tenacity in preparing the final manuscript.

Special thanks are extended to Eunice Lambert for information on Cherokee pottery; to William S. Fowler for permission to reproduce his fine illustrations of Northeast pottery; to Jean Jacques Rivard for assistance in obtaining information and illustrations; to Janet Friedman for insight into the Federal role in archaeology and suggestions for sources of information on pottery; to Charlie R. Steen for information on ceramics of the Pajarito Plateau; to Stuart Struever for suggestions on information sources; to June DuBois for use of photographs from her book *W. R. Leigh*; to Frank G. Hathaway, the Los Angeles Athletic Club for permission to reproduce W. R. Leigh's "Pool at Oraibi"; to Sandra L. Brizee of the San Diego Museum of Man for patience and thorough search for specific photographs; to Ken Hedges for information on pottery of Southern California; to C. W. Kirby, National Museums of Canada, for assistance on prehistoric Canadian pottery; to Chuck Dailey, Institute of American Indian Art and Myles Libhart, Indian Arts and Crafts Board for information on contemporary ceramics; to Philip Hitchcock, California State University, Sacramento for loan of photographs; to Gayle F. Carlson, Nebraska State Historical Society for selection of many fine photographs; and to numerous Pueblo potters who have so generously shared their enthusiasm, time, and information over the past several years.

Appreciation is extended to the following institutions and museums which offered photographs and/or information: Massachusetts Archaeological Society; Los Alamos Scientific Laboratory; U.S. Department of the Interior, Pecos National Monument, Institute of American Indian Arts, Indian Arts and Crafts Board, of the National Park Service; Smithsonian Institution; Milwaukee Public Museum; Nebraska Historical Society; Utah Historical Society; Lincoln (Nebraska) Museum; Ohio Historical Society; Illinois State Museum; San Diego Museum of Man; Santa Fe Railway; Public Archives of Canada; National Museum of Canada, and the Museum of New Mexico.

I should also like to extend a special thanks to the following galleries, shops, and private individuals who provided photographs at their own expense or permitted their collections to be photographed: Leon Hodge, Indian Jewelry Center, Sacramento; Marsha Adams, Bien Mur, Albuquerque; Forrest Fenn and Elizabeth Zedlicka, Fenn Galleries, Ltd., Santa Fe; Al Anthony, Adobe Gallery, Albuquerque; Charles Cleland and Richard Cleland, Pueblo One Indian Arts, Scottsdale; Barry Powell; Audrey Greenough; Macolm and Jean Gross; Marguerite L. Kernaghan; Peter Pilles; Nancy Page; David Ichelson; Blake Gahagan; Jerry and Dorothy Guinand, Spencer Esplin; Robert LaPerriere; Jim Grenwelge and Ike Lovato.

Two photographers, William Klein and William Ciesla, who provided high quality photographs at their own expense are especially acknowleged.

And finally, I should like to express my gratitude to Dan Alexander of Books Americana for his patience and for making this publication possible.

A word about pricing — the values provided in this 1984 supplement are average trade prices. The prices should be used as a guide only as several factors influence market values. These factors are discussed on page 19 of *American Indian Pottery*. Prices are omitted for all prehistoric pottery and pottery in museums.

May, 1984

John W. Barry
Davis, California

INTRODUCTION

Archaeologists since Thomas Jefferson[1] have been studying prehistoric man in North America and the pottery he left as tangible evidence of his presence. Ceramics were well established in North America before the time of Christ, and developed to a high level of technical and artistic excellence particularly in the Southwest.

It is generally accepted that pottery was in use by 2500 BC, (Martin et. al. 1947). By 200 BC, it had achieved a high level of development as represented by the artistically executed pottery produced by the Hohokam-Mimbres cultures of the Southwest. Generally pottery progressed throughout North America concurrently with the development of the agrarian cultures.

Ceramics is an ancient world art form, possibly dating back 10,000 years. Early Eyptian pottery has been dated back 7,000 years while Chinese pottery may have a more recent age of 4,000 years. Undoubtedly, early immigrants to North America via the Bering Straits brought pottery with them or the knowledge to produce pottery. Additionally, archaeologists have found pottery in North America with similarities to Asiatic types. As research intensifies in search of the First American, the mystery of the origin of pottery in North American may be unraveled.

It seems reasonable to assume that early man would discover and pursue the manufacture of ceramics when the opportunity and need arose. Early man in North America undoubtedly had the capacity to produce ceramics. The earliest positive evidence of man in North America suggests technical achievements which require major skills and creativity. The beautifully shaped Folsom and Sandia stone artifacts are examples. Man's survival was dependent upon adapting to his environment in search of food, water, and shelter. When he had the need for a container he found a natural container or he made one from available materials. One opportunity undoubtedly occurred during the transition from nomadic hunter and gatherer to farmer. Once life became more residential, household items could be expanded. Certainly, we can see this in our own way of life. The longer we reside in the same location, the more items we acquire with little concern for packing and transportation to another location. Was early man any different? I think not.

His agricultural products and harvested foods were best when cooked. They also required storage. Some type of container was needed for these purposes. Various methods could be used—A hollowed-out rock or log, bark, skins, shells, gourds, baskets, depressions in clay soil, or preferably, a clay container. At first unfired clay containers were probably used near fire. Soon the benefits of baking the clay container were discovered by accident or by curiosity. The probability of this discovery spontaneously and independently by isolated groups seems overwhelming, and it seems reasonable to support the suggestion that this discovery was hit upon at different times by different people. This is not to contradict the probable introduction of pottery technology northward from Mexico and Central America. But we must recognize that the pottery had an early development in the Archaic and Early Woodland Cultures of the Northeast as by 1500 BC pottery was in use. To further support the spontaneous idea, let's make an observation of children at play.

Mud is one of the favorite play medias for pre-school children. Most children enjoy this form of play and if permitted to play unsupervised with mud they can show a considerable amount of creativity. Disc, spheres, bowls, figures, and even coils are produced from mud. It is common to observe them producing coils similar to those used to produce a bowl. Some children will use the coil to form a bowl, smoothing the coils, and decorate the surface with their fingernails or a stick. Progressing then to kindergarten, children will continue to make small bowls with clay, following two of the ancient methods used by prehistoric man to make pottery— the molding and the coiling methods.

In the Americas, pottery art reached its highest development in Mexico, Central America, and Peru. Glazing of the entire pot was not used but the overall technical aspects of the pottery equalled, and in many cases exceeded that of the pottery produced in Europe and Asia. The influence of this pottery art from the south (Mexico and Central America) reached the inhabitants of the territory which is now Arizona and New Mexico. As distances increase northward and eastward from the Southwest there is less evidence of influence.

The beautiful modern day polychrome pottery from the Southwest shares the greatest popularity with students and collectors alike. The gray, black, or brown wares of the other areas, even though equal in technical execution, have not shared a comparable popularity.

To the archaeologists, pottery is an excellent correlator much as a trilobite fossil might suggest an

---

[1]Thomas Jefferson, Third President of the United States, was the first American to conduct a scientific excavation of an archaeological site. He published his finds, ''Notes on the State of Virginia'' in 1781. His systematic work resulted in the stratum approach (stratigraphy) to archeological excavation which would become the basic approach to field archaeology.

oil bearing strata. No single artifact provides as many clues to prehistoric life as pottery. It is a definite tangible artifact unquestionably manufactured by human hands. It is usually found at its location of last use in association with other evidence of human activity. Traces of pottery provide the unwritten record of those cultures which relied upon ceramics for the utility purposes of cooking, storage and gathering; and for ceremonial purposes and for trading. There may be a temptation by archaeologists to conclude too much from pottery, particularly when studying differences between two closely related cultures; however, it is the single most important evidence available. More is known about the pottery-producing cultures of North America than about other cultures without a pottery tradition. Pottery has an amazing resistance to weathering elements of nature. The painted designs which have been fixed on the pottery by firing withstand centuries of weathering. Quantity, quality, shape, size and variety of types of pottery help the archaeologist to fill in the puzzle of relating and studying the sequence and progression of cultures.

As an example, Anasazi pottery of the Southwest reveals considerable variation from period to period, sub-culture to sub-culture, and even village to village. This variation is evident today when one examines the historic and modern pottery styles produced by ancestors of the Anasazi. The art of pottery making in ancient times progressed and declined as it has in modern times and probably for some of the same reasons. It has been suggested that the prehistoric potter made her best pots during difficult times to appease the gods. Therefore, pottery has served the student of early man in studying those who left no written record. A study of modern Indian pottery and potters provides an opportunity to understand past and present cultures. If we were to observe and study the modern day Pueblo potter we might better understand the culture of their ancestors. The modern day setting provides opportunities to study and to understand the past.

Methods of Production

North American Indians used five methods to make pottery. None employed a potters' wheel or anything resembling a wheel.

1. Coil Method. Rolls of clay are built upon a clay base in a spiral manner. The pot is developed by successive coils and the sides are smoothed by a piece of gourd, corncob, shell, or smooth stone. The Hopi and Rio Grande Pueblos use this method today.

2. Coil Method with Paddle and Anvil. This method is similar to the coil method except that coils are rarely applied spirally. A paddle and anvil are used to thin and compress the seams. The rancheria and prehistoric people of the Middle and Lower Gila River districts of Arizona used this technique. The present day Maricopas followed this tradition.

3. Paddle and Anvil Method. No coils are used but the paddle and anvil were used as described above. Some Northern Plains Indians used this method.

4. Modeling Method. Eskimos probably used this method which consisted simply of modeling clay in the desired form.

5. Molded in Basket Method. In this method a layer of clay is molded to the interior of the basket. During the firing process, the basket is lost producing a pot with identations of the basket on the exterior. This is probably one of the first methods used to produce pottery in the Southwest.

Maria and Julian Martinez posed in 1932 for a series of photographs (Figs 1-6) to illustrate various aspects of the pottery making sequence.

Selection and preparation of the clay are basic to making quality pottery. The potter or her family collects clay at sites which have been known to the Pueblo and to the family for centuries. Likewise, sources of the tempering agent are collected locally unless ground potsherds are used. Collecting these materials may be considered somewhat of a sacred ritual by some potters but this has not been established in modern times. For whatever the reason, potters are generally rather vague about the location of their clay pits.

After the clay is collected it is cleaned, dried, and pulverized by grinding. The fine particles are then mixed with a tempering agent and water, made into a paste and left to cure. Some Pueblos or potters mix the clean, dry clay directly with water and screen out the impurities. A tempering agent is used with the clay during this process to reduce strain and pressures during drying and during firing of the pot. Temper, being a non-plastic material, allows for more even heating and cooling of the plastic clay by preventing 100% binding of the clay particles. Thus, tempering agents reduce the chance of uneven strain and breakage while the pot is being dried and fired.

In the coil method, a base is formed either free hand or by molding the clay paste in a dish or small

Pottery Making Sequence by Marie Martinez

1. In this step Marie Martinez of San Il-defonso Pueblo, is cleaning the clay particles by letting the wind remove organic material.

2. This photo shows her pulverizing dried clay with mano and metate.

3. Marie is demonstrating the initial step of the coil method to make a pot. She is forming the base by molding in a saucer. Note the prepared clay and scrapers to her right which will be used later to smooth the pots such as those in the foreground.

4. Forming a symmetrical coil.

5. Placing the coil on the lip of the base.

6. Julian and Marie Martinez, San Ildefonso Pueblo, are firing their pottery in the traditiona manner. The fire is smothered with manure to produce the classical black ware.

Photos 1-6 reproduced from a series of 1932 lantern slides, courtesy Philip Hitchcock, California State University, Sacramento.

bowl. The walls are built-up by adding coils successively while the potter's hands are working constantly smoothing the coils on both the inner and outer walls. Vessel walls are thinned possibly by a piece of wood or gourd rind. On slipped pottery, a clay base slip is applied by painting on the outer surface. Occasionally all surfaces are painted. Before the slip dries, a smooth pebble is used to polish the surface. After polishing, the pot is allowed to dry. The pot then may be decorated with vegetal and/or mineral base paints before firing.

There are two types of firing processes commonly referred to as oxidation and reduction. In the oxidation process the fire, having access to air, burns hot and clean, while in the reduction process the fire is cooler and fueled with animal manure to produce carbon. Red ware and lighter colored pots are produced by the oxidation method while the popular black pots from Santa Clara and San Ildefonso are fired by the reduction process. Black-ware results from the release of carbon from manure which is us-ed to smother the fire. Firing may last for up to three hours and may reach temperatures up to 1500° F.

A skillful potter can produce a small simple pot in about two hours exclusive of drying and firing, which may take at least another 15 hours. Large pots require several weeks to complete, depending upon the amount of decoration and polishing. Large ollas such as those made by Margaret Tofoya and her daughter, Virginia Ebelacker at Santa Clara Pueblo, are examples of the latter.

Today, traditional Pueblo pottery is made essentially in the same manner as prehistoric pottery. Women usually are the potters, although assistance is often provided by son and husband in decorating the pottery. In recent years, several men have become known as outstanding ceramic artists. Examples are Tony Da, Robert Tenorio, Elmer Gates, Mike Daniel, Carlos Dunlap, and Joseph Lonewolf. Maria Martinez's husband Julian was probably the first modern day male potter. He decorated many of Maria's pots. Pottery making is usually learned from mother or grandmother.

Marketing of Contemporary Pottery

Buyers of native American art have changed over the past decade and the acceptance of this art form has taken a new orientation. Previously, it was generally collected as a curiosity or as a souvenir. There was minimal interest in the artist, his history, or the achievement associated with the object. The artist responded accordingly and provided what he or she thought the buyer wanted. There was little insight provided as to the historical and technical aspects of the object much less the more intangible motivations of the artist. Ceramics were no exception. Artists in need of a continual outlet frequently told the buyer what they thought the buyer wanted to hear. The potter was careful not to reveal his or her inner feelings about the pottery. There was little in the past to support rapport and trust with non-Indians.

In retrospect, one can understand their reticence. There were, however, several non-Indians who gained the trust of potters and developed strong friendships.

The ceramic artist and the consumer are in transition. More pottery is being produced today than at any other time since prehistoric times and it represents a great range of styles. Each year new creations are presented at numerous exhibitions and galleries and are received with enthusiasm by collectors. The traditionalist is still seeking the older styles while others are interested in modern or abstract ceramics. Consumers are communicating their feelings directly to the artists through these public showings and the artists are responding with creativity and technical excellence. The casual buyer is becoming less important within the ceramic market.

Indian pottery is marketed by a variety of outlets and methods. The uniqueness of pottery requires marketing methods which differ from other Indian arts and crafts. The creator of the pot usually is identified with the piece of pottery whether it is being marketed by a museum, a trader, a retailer, an auctioneer, or by one of the Indian cooperatives. No two pieces are alike as each is built by coiling and decorated by hand. The potter's wheel was never used by the North American Indian. A specific size, shape, and design cannot be ordered. The potter is not a duplicator; each pot is an unique creation although differences might be slight. Each potter has his or her own style which often is readily identifiable.

The single most important event in the

marketing of Pueblo pottery occurs annually in New Mexico at the Santa Fe Indian Market. The Market is sponsored by Southwestern Association of Indian Affairs (SWAIA), a group of citizens dedicated to the advancement of the arts and crafts. People from various tribal affiliations are eligible to exhibit but they must meet a high set of standards established by the SWAIA. At the 1979 Market, there were 152 registered pottery exhibitors representing 17 of the 20 Pueblos. Each registered pottery exhibitor may represent several potters from a single family. Of the 357 official exhibitors at the Market, approximately 45% were potters. There were no potters representing the Pueblos of Picuris, Taos, and Sandia. The situation was similar at the 1980 Market, there were 359 official booths, 41% or 168 of which were potters. Seventeen of the 20 Pueblos were represented with none from Taos, Sandia, and San Felipe.

The Market is significant for several reasons. At a single event, one can view the current state-of-the-art and development of Pueblo pottery. The Market provides a unique opportunity to study pottery traditions from a single Pueblo, and to compare developments and trends among Pueblos. New prices are established and the potters can test the market with their new creations. The potter is instantly rewarded and recognized for his or her artistic ability through the awards presented and through the prices received for the pots. All buyers compete on an equal basis for the pottery whether they are tourists, traders, dealers, collectors, or museum agents.

Museum and other public and private institutions have sponsored an increasing number of pottery exhibits in recent years. Pottery usually is available for sale during these exhibits. Such events have served both the potter and the public in promoting communications and enhancing appreciation and recognition of Indian pottery. Additionally, exhibits provide monetary incentives to the artist. These institutions usually maintain an inventory of pottery made by the exhibiting artists.

Galleries have become popular for one-artist pottery shows. These are presented in the same manner as shows for other types of artists, sometimes utilizing a reception for special limited guests and collectors. Shows of this nature have proved to be a

7. Sale booths at the 1979 Santa Fe Indian Market. Most noted potters are represented at this prestigious market.

mutual benefit to the artist and to the gallery. The potter-artists have come to recognize the essential role of the gallery in promoting their work outside their home area. Today's buyer of art enjoys interacting with the artists.

The large, 50 to 200 dealer-exhibitor shows, popular during the last decade, have played their part in bringing pottery to collectors who otherwise would not have an opportunity to see and purchase a variety of pottery. As a means of marketing pottery, these shows have been unpredictable and subject to economic conditions and other factors existing at the time. There is evidence that shows of this type are becoming less popular than in previous years.

The individual Indian-type shop which carries a variety of Indian arts and crafts is the primary retail outlet for pottery. These shops may be privately owned or in public museums. Outside of the pottery producing areas, such as outside Arizona and New Mexico, more pottery is sold through these shops than through any other means. These retail outlets usually are supplied by traders who specialize in pottery from certain potters or specific pottery producing Pueblos and tribes. The shop owner frequently depends upon the trader to keep him updated on developments in pottery while a few of the owners make annual or semi-annual buying trips to purchase pottery.

The Indian trader, one who purchases pottery directly from the potter, plays a very important function in promoting and distributing pottery beyond the pottery-producing areas. The trader of the 20th Century is essentially an agent of the potter who competes for quality pottery with other traders. He is a professional whose business is dependent upon honest dealings with the potter and with his customers. Problems which do occur from time to time are due to misunderstandings and are compounded by fluctuating market conditions. The trader's job always involves long travel distances, uncertainties of supply, and frustration in anticipation of his customer's needs.

Many potters sell directly from their homes. A few potters prefer this method and market exclusively in this manner. One may pay the same or even more at the potter's home than he might pay at a retail shop. Price is set by what the market will bear. But the price is insignificant when compared to the cost of traveling to the potter. On the other hand, the reward of meeting and talking with the artist is priceless to the inquisitive buyer and to the collector.

Most potters are more than willing to visit and explain the process of making pottery. They usually have pots in various stages of production and depending upon timing, you may see a group of pots being removed from a primitive firing pit, although some potters will not permit observation of the firing pro-

cedure. The potter will show you the clay, polishing stone, and pots awaiting delivery to customers. It is advisable to make an appointment before you visit. Winter is the best time to visit and make purchases. At that time, you will not be competing with other tourists and various public shows, and markets which require a large inventory. Potters will also keep their better pieces for those shows. I have met scores of people who recall vividly meeting potters such as Maria Martinez, Margaret Tafoya, and Frogwoman. Their excitement and fascination in purchasing a pot directly from a famous potter is still evident after 30 or 40 years! Undoubtedly, this method of marketing will continue in spite of projected changes in travel patterns. If one chooses this method of purchasing pottery, protocol calls for an appointment and some restraint in questioning the potter unless it is apparent that questioning is welcomed. A genuine approach will result in voluntary answers. Some Reservations require that you check in with the Reservation officials or Pueblo governor's office before visiting potters within Reservations boundaries.

Reservation shops and Indian cooperative guilds sell a fair amount of pottery. They provide an excellent outlet for potters entering the market and a service to the tourist visiting the reservations. Because the Indians respect all pottery, their inventory might include pottery from several areas. Examples of the Reservation shop are Bien Mur at Sandia Pueblo near Albuquerque, New Mexico; Hopi Cooperative Guild at Second Mesa, Arizona; and Gila River Arts and Crafts Center, Sacaton, Arizona.

Most Pueblos and Reservations also sponsor annual shows during the summer months, although some with strong local markets have shows during the non-tourist season. Pottery is usually prominently featured at the all-Indian shows.

Santa Fe, in addition to hosting the Santa Fe Indian Market, is the primary trade center for Pueblo pottery. Its proximity to the Pueblos provides a ready market for Pueblo potters who wholesale to shops. Museums, shops, and traders are active in marketing pottery to all areas of the United States from Santa Fe, Albuquerque, and Gallup, New Mexico.

As with any other commodity, price is dictated by supply and demand. Quality pottery, whether it is traditional or non-traditional in style, has consistently been in demand and commands the higher price. Once a potter has become recognized, her pottery will usually be in demand and its price will rise proportionally with that demand. She will be sensitive to the need to improve quality and may create new styles while not over-producing. Prices of quality pottery in recent years have appreciated in excess of

25% per year but quality is the key to the economic balance of supply, demand, and price.

Another recent marketing technique is the Indian auction. This method has become popular in recent years since initial successes of a few auctions involving some major collections of Indian arts and crafts. A variety of pottery types are usually involved representing prehistoric, historic, and modern types; however, the volume of pots relative to other items usually is small. Auctions do not represent a significant marketing method for pottery; however this may change.

Ruth L. Bunzel (Bunzel 1972) reported in her field studies of 1924-1925 on Pueblo pottery activity of the Southwest. It is through published observations, made directly in the field by researchers such as Bunzel, that we have an opportunity to track changes in ceramic arts and to gather information on a particular industry. At the time of her observations, from 1924-1925, pottery was being produced at the Pueblos of Santa Clara, San Ildefonso, Zia, Santa Ana, Zuni, Santo Domingo, Cochiti, Isleta, Acoma, Laguna, and the Hopi First Mesa village of Tusayan. Absent from this list are the Pueblos of Sandia, San Felipe, Jemez, Tesuque, Nambe, Pojoaque, and San Juan; it is presumed that if there was any significant pottery production at these Pueblos it would have been know to Bunzel. Ceramic art was near extinction at Zia, Santa Clara, Santa Ana, and Luguna. The Pueblos of Santo Domingo, Isleta and Cochiti were making primarily an inexpensive souvenir for tourists while at Acoma, San Ildefonso, and Hopi First Mesa pottery was a profitable industry. Pottery was made for utilitarian use at Acoma and Zuni at that time.

Information on past marketing activities and pricing of modern pottery is nearly non-existent. A few catalogs since the turn of the century list pottery; however, these are restricted to publication by only a few dealers and are extremely rare today. Ruth L. Bunzel (Bunzel 1929) obtained price information on pottery from six Pueblos which is provided for comparison on a relative basis with those presented in the contemporary section.:

"In 1924 the following prices for pottery prevailed at various Pueblos:

Zuni. *Pottery is not ordinarily made for sale. However, a new or slightly used water jar, twelve inches high, brings the owner two or three dollars. Pottery that has been traded against credit or pawned with storekeepers is sometimes sold cheaper than this, which tends to depress the general level of prices. Large prices are asked for old and rare pieces; but the owner, if temporarily pressed for money, will not refuse offers of less.*

Laguna. *The principal trade is in small pieces which are sold on the road to automobile tourists, and bring the maker from fifteen to fifty cents each.*

Acoma. *A large water jar brings about $1.50; small pieces twenty-five to fifty cents, when sold direct to tourists; prices are probably lower for traders.*

Hopi. *It is impossible to state what a potter receives. The method of marketing operates very unfavorably to the potter. The villages are very remote from the market; consequently the whole output is disposed of to Tom Pavatea, the local trader, in return for credit at the store. A woman will bring in her output of two weeks, consisting of some fifty pieces of various sizes. She has an outstanding debt at the store, and the value of the pottery is used to reduce this debt. The woman has no clear conception of what she receives for her work; and Tom is reticent on this subject. Tom gets for a water jar by Nampeyo two to five dollars, depending on the size—the five dollar size being exceptionally large for any place. A twelve inch bowl by Nampeyo, seventy-five cents. The work of other potters is cheaper. Small pieces being from fifteen to fifty cents each. Higher prices prevail on the mesa, potters realizing the extent to which they can fleece the unwary purchaser.*

San Idlefonso. *Pottery is marketed on the same basis as artistic products among ourselves. Prices are conditioned by quality of craftsmanship and the fame of the maker. The work of the most famous potters is handled on a strictly commission basis by Santa Fe traders,—the only case of this kind of trading in Indian products with which the writer is familiar. A small bowl of decorated black ware by Maria Martinez brings from three to six dollars. Large and unusual pieces, such as prayer-meal bowls, vases, bring up to twelve dollars. Other potters get less for their work. A small globular bowl, six inches in diameter, by Tonita Roybal, can be purchased for three dollars; a flat bowl twelve inches in diameter, for the same price. Prices at the village are slightly lower.*

Santo Domingo. *A fourteen inch bowl by Monica Silva, decorated black ware, $1.50; a full size water jar in polychrome, $1 to $1.50."*

The future of all Indian arts and crafts is dependent upon the attitude, motivations and changing culture of the Indians. Pottery is no exception. Today there are several full-time potters making a living as ceramic artists. They are motivated by economic benefits as well as by a need for recognition of their accomplishments. As long as there is an appreciation of pottery, it will continue to be produced. Quality pottery by recognized potters probably will continue to appreciate in value. Historic and prehistoric pottery will become part of institutional collections as more private collections are donated to public institutions. Styles will continue to change with the imagination of the artists. This creativity is essential to the future vitality of this art. The vitality of this art form is dependent upon change and excellence. The artists must be permitted to express themselves from within or there will be no art. The consuming public should encourage and accept the creative imagination of native Americans in their pursuit of ceramics.

Value of Contemporary Pottery

Nothing is constant but change. Prices and values of pottery are best represented by this anonymous quotation. Contrary to popular belief the price of a fine pot can decline even though in recent years the demand for quality pottery has been strong. The price of Indian pottery as an average or individually as of 1980 has never been higher.

The usual supply and demand scenario is that prices will climb to a level which balances the number of buyers. At that point the price will level off and possibly even decline depending upon many factors. One of the main controlling factors is the potter's willingness to sell and this would be influenced by her economic needs. If the potter is dependent upon income she might be more inclined to accept the bid of the buyer. On the other hand, if she has reached a level of confidence in public acceptance of her pottery, and is not dependent upon a steady income, she probably will maintain her prices at a set level and possibly reduce production.

Factors which can influence the sell price:

1. Supply and scarcity
2. Popularity of the potter
3. Popularity of the Pueblo/tribe
4. Aesthestic features of the pot
5. Overall quality and condition
6. Family tradition
7. Marketing and promotion skills of the potter, trader or agent
8. Participation and recognition of potter in major Indian shows and exhibits
9. Traditional conformity or creativity
10. Prices resulting from public auctions
11. Geographic location
12. Economic conditions
13. Salesperson's knowledge of Indian ceramics

The above factors influence the values assigned to contemporary pottery in this book. Therefore, the price tag on a pot should be expected to vary widely from shop to shop, location to location, etc.

Prices of collector pieces are reflected in table 1 on page 20. This is a listing of pottery exhibited at the Institute of American Indian Museum, Santa Fe, New Mexico, in 1978.

Table 1 - Pottery exhibited at Institute of American Indian Museum 1978.

Potter	Pueblo/Tribe	Title	Price
MARIE G. ROMERO	Jemez	"Hunter" Ceramic	$200.00
		"Small Nativity" Ceramic (Set of 10)	$300.00
		"Paper Bread Making" Ceramic	$200.00
		"Wedding Vase" Ceramic	$400.00
		"Storyteller" Ceramic	$400.00
		"Large Nativity" Ceramic (Set of 2)	$250.00
		"Canteen With Clown" Ceramic	$200.00
ROBERT TENORIO	Santo Domingo	"Small Bowl" Ceramic	$85.00
		"Small Vase" Ceramic	$85.00
		"Medium Bowl" Ceramic	$200.00
		"Large Bowl" Ceramic	$600.00
		"Large Vase" Ceramic	$900.00
		"Medium Bowl" Ceramic	$200.00
		"Medium Vase" Ceramic	$500.00
LAURA GACHUPIN	Jemez	"Kiva Bowl" Ceramic	$325.00
		"Small Bowl" Ceramic	$225.00
		"Turtle Vase" Ceramic	$325.00
		"Turtle Bowl" Ceramic	$350.00
		"Vase With Turtle" "Lid"	$350.00
		"Owl Bowl" Ceramic	$350.00
BLUE CORN	San Ildefonso	"Medium Bowl" Polychrome	$1,250.00
		"Large Bowl" Polychrome	$1,575.00
		"Small Plate" Polychrome	$175.00
		"Small Vase" Polychrome	$425.00
		"Black Vase" Ceramic	$650.00
MAXINE GACHUPIN	Jemez	"Small Owl" Ceramic Sculpture	$35.00
		"Large Owl" Ceramic Sculpture	$50.00
		"Kiva" Ceramic	$600.00
		"Vase" Ceramic	$200.00
TSE-PE & DORA	San Ildefonso	"Water Jar-With Carved Serpent and Silver Lid" Ceramic	$2,700.00
		'Seed Jar-Designs On Three Sides" Ceramic	$2,400.00
		"Storage Jar Etched Serpent, Bear Fetish Lid" Ceramic	$1,800.00
		"Fruit Bowl With Serpent" Ceramic	$1,500.00
		"Bear Fetish With Silver Flint" Ceramic	$400.00
ART & MARTHA HAUNGOOAH	Kiowa/Santa Clara	"Prarie Chicken Small Pot" Ceramic	$300.00
		"Quail Pot" Ceramics	$200.00
		"Serpent Small Pot" Ceramics	$250.00
		"Medium Pot" Ceramic	$900.00

Selecting A Piece Of Pottery

Your intitial reaction to a piece of pottery should guide your selection. If the piece is aesthetically pleasing initially, in all probability it will remain so if it satisfies other secondary characteristics. Disregard price if possible, particularly if you are looking for collector pieces. A collector piece is one made by a famous potter, shows unique technical and artistic qualities, and probably commands a relatively high price. Look for cracks which occur during the firing and cooling process. Some are readily detectable while others are very inconspicious. If possible, examine the interior. Natural lighting is best for examing a pot. Fine cracks and crazing can be overlooked in artificial light.

It is best to avoid any pot which has a crack or chip as it will always be of less value. Experienced collectors have their own method of testing for soundness. One common test is to tap the rim of the pot with your fingernail as you would to evaluate a piece of crystal. There should be a resonant sound, not a thud. Symmetry or overall evenness is important and the pot should sit tall, not lopsided. Polished pottery such as Santa Clara Pueblo blackware should be smooth, even textured, and have few facets. Blackware also should be black or a gun metal black but never brown. Polishing inside the bowl and on the bottom represents additional effort of the potter which usually is not encountered on average grade pottery. The design should be symmetrical, lines relatively even, and designs balanced. Condition is important; look for scratches, chips, etc. Note that when handling a pot, one should place one hand on the bottom and the other grasping the side. Also it is advisable to remove jewelry which could scratch the surface. Never hold a pot solely by the rim.

Generally each Pueblo or pottery-producing Reservation has a tradition style which is culturally acceptable. What might be acceptable or even necessary to one Pueblo may be entirely unacceptable to another. An example would be black fire clouds on Taos pottery which reflects higher firing temperatures necessary for utilization purposes. These would be unacceptable, as an example, on fine Santa Clara redware. Round bottom Navajo pots also serve a purpose for open-fire cooking while a San Ildefonso pot with a round bottom would be unacceptable for any purpose.

One cannot generalize about color. Many contemporary potters are experimenting with various color media and color combinations. Colors on traditional pottery, however, should be consistent with the pottery traditon of the Pueblo. This is particularly true with polychrome pottery. As an example, orange should not have a pinkish cast and white should not be gray. Most pots are painted before firing, a process which fixes the color. Before purchasing, try to ascertain the method of painting. If the paint will rub off such as on the pot shown in Fig. 8, reconsider your purchase. There are a few noted potters who are experiencing difficulties with native paints not affixing to the pot during firing. The paint, particularly black, will rub off or smear on such pots. Potters must continue to experiment and while they are under pressure to use ancient methods, technical problems undoubtedly will occur when all methods are not transfered or passed on to the next generation.

Look for small pits on the surface. (Figs. 9 & 10) Some pots from Acoma, Jemez, Zia, and San Ildefonso and possibly other Pueblos show evidence of pitting caused by impurities in the clay. This is no reflection upon the skill of the potter as potters of all skill levels can experience this problem. But depending upon the severity, it may affect the pot's appeal and value. Unfortunately, pitting or "spall off" may occur weeks after firing. The source providing the pot should be willing to replace it. Depending upon the type slip, it is possible for the potter to patch the pits.

Some of the traditional type pots from the Navajo, Zia, Taos, Picuris, Acoma and Santo Domingo are utilitarian while most pots from other Pueblos are strictly decorative. Your dealer or the potter will discuss this with you. However, regardless of the type, it is advisable not to use the pot as a water container. Results of such use are shown in Fig. 11.

Properly seasoned pots from Taos and Picuris are excellent for oven use. Although some Indians may use their native pottery for special uses, cost usually dictates that the pot be displayed as a piece of art and not used as a container for food or cooking.

Unfortunately some potters from Pueblos and Reservations known to produce strictly traditional pottery are resorting to non-traditional techinques. This includes use of the potter's wheel, molds, commercial paints, and electric kilns. This is objectionable to the traditionalist who might argue that these practices will lead to a general decline in pottery. Others will argue that such practices are objectionable only if these modern methods are used to simulate traditional wares. The consumer and cultural pressures at the Reservation will probably keep these practices in check for traditional wares. If the practice is open and the pottery is marketed for what it is, there is no problem (Fig. 12). The potter following this practice has a moral responsibility to inform the buyer if he or she used these methods to produce an otherwise traditional-appearing pot. It would seem more appropriate for these potters, however, to use modern methods to create ceramics of their own conception.

8. The design on this pot has been rubbed off. The potter apparently used improper paints. Examine painted pottery carefully before purchase.

9. Example of pitting or spall-off on this San Ildefonso Pueblo bowl.

10. Close-up view of pitting on an Acoma pot.

11. This polychrome vase was used as a water container. Although some Pueblo pottery will hold water, it is a good rule not to use collector-type Indian pottery as a container.

12. Example of pottery made using commercial paints and electric kiln. This pot was made by South Dakota Sioux who made little or no pottery in historic times. Pottery of this type sells for less than $50.

13. The turtle on this canteen has been jarred loose—note the discontinuity in the slip at the base of turtle. Pottery with appliqued designs must be handled with care.

14. Varnish has been placed on the polished rim of this ca 1950 San Juan Pueblo olla.

15. This vase shows shelf damage caused by a collision with another pot. In this example the slip has chipped off.

16. The base of this fine bowl shows evidence of damage due to lifting of the slip when price tags were removed. Price and descriptive information should be placed on a card and not attached directly to the pot.

Generally it is difficult to ascertain whether or not a pot has been fired in the traditional manner or in an electric kiln. There are clues. If the pot seems very brittle which suggests high temperature firing, it may have been kiln-fired. On the other hand, if the pot is blackware or has a fire cloud, it probably was fired in an outdoor pit.

The technique of applique has resulted in problems. If the applique (lizards, turtles, etc.) are not properly applied, they can become dislodged with ease. The canteen in Fig. 13 illustrates this point. Consumers should be aware of possible problems with applique pots.

Owners of pottery can and do subject their pottery to a variety of deleterious treatments. Besides chips, cracks, abrasions, and destruction of the pot by using it as a water container, some owners are known to varnish or even paint their pots. Varnishing and sometimes even painting might not be noticeable at first glance. Note the rim on the San Juan pot (Fig. 14) which has been varnished. Pottery which has seen such abuse loses most of its value.

One other caution is blackware which has had black shoe polish rubbed in the red clay. This simulation of blackware has been reported at one Pueblo, and if the report is correct, it probably is an isolated occurrence. The Pueblos and tribes are concerned about any misrepresentation and undoubtedly will deal with problems of this nature.

Appraisers, museums, and other institutions which might appraise or exchange prehistoric and contemporary ceramics should be alert to reproductions and fakes. As with any rare item when there is a strong market and the price of a collectable rises, counterfeiting occures. As an example, designs have been painted inside prehistoric bowls to fake Mimbres pottery. And signatures of famous potters have been placed on contemporary pottery.

There is a wide choice and informed buyers will make fewer mistakes in their selections. If you are inexperienced, buy from a knowledgeable dealer, museum or a potter.

Care and Handling

Proper care and handling of Indian ceramics are important considerations to enjoying this art form. As with other art and antiques, condition affects value—almost always. Present and future values of Indian pottery likewise will be dictated by condition. There are a few considerations and precautions for maintaining pottery in good condition and preventing damage from mishandling.

Most pots are soft because of low temperature firing, and none have a protective glaze. Therefore they are susceptible to abrasion and scratching. Most damage of this nature results from collision with other shelf items (Fig. 15), or scratching with rings or other objects. Careless handling can result in marring the surface. Another common problem is abrasion on the base which may result in obliterating signatures. This can be especially distracting on collector pieces. Abrasions can be avoided by placing the pot on cloth pads. The use of gummed labels on the base for pricing or identification also should be avoided. Labels will either discolor the pot or cling to the slip, and when removed, take part of the slip with it (Fig. 16). Tags with appropriate information can be placed inside the pot and sometimes cotton string attached to handles can be used to hold tags.

Pottery should not be used as containers for liquids or objects (Fig. 11). Liquids will discolor the surface and cause the slip to separate from the underlying clay. Handle only one pot at a time and use both hands to grasp the sides; avoid picking up a pot by its rim. Pottery should be dusted by using a clean soft cloth or feather duster. Most quality traditional Indian pottery can be cleaned with a damp cloth or sponge. Consult a museum specialist before using any cleaning compound.

Lighted display cabinets are an attractive way to store, protect and enjoy your collection. Lights can produce high interior temperatures and one should be careful that excessive heat does not crack glass shelves. Properly designed cases call for tempered plate glass, ventilation and fluorescent lights.

Record keeping is an important aspect of collecting pottery. You should record name of potter, location, appropriate remarks made by the potter or dealer, and date purchased. This will help also to authenticate your pot in future years, particularly when the record card is accompanied by a photograph.

Repair and restoration of pottery requires a specialist. Most museums and archaeologists can advise on sources of repair and restoration of ceramics. Contemporary pottery loses its value if broken or seriously damaged making repairs questionable. Prehistoric and historic pottery, however, is repaired and restored frequently, enhancing its desireability and value.

Stored pottery should be wrapped in soft white tissue paper or a soft cloth. Air-tight plastic bags may cause condensation and result in damage. Place several inches of padding between stored pots and label the exterior of the container including all the contents.

Classification

North American Indian pottery is coventionally classified chronologically[2]. The main divisional classes are Prehistoric, Historic, Modern or Contemporary.

Prehistoric Pottery. Classification of prehistoric pottery, particularly that found east of the Mississippi River, is best accomplished geographically because of simultaneous development in various geographical areas. For those interested in a more in-depth study of pottery produced by various cultures, books such as Martin, Quimby and Colliers' book, *Indians Before Columbus* should be reviewed[3].

SOUTHWEST

Anasazi Culture

Modified Basket maker 450-750 AD - First pottery, indented, corrugated, sun dried, some made in baskets, later fired and temper added to clay.

Pueblo I and Pueblo II Development Pueblo Period. 750-1100 AD - Pottery improved, period of experimentation.

Pueblo III - Classic Pueblo Period. 1100-1300 AD - Pottery reached its peak of development, more specialized, distinctive types from each area such as Chaco and Mesa Verde, numerous sub-divisions.

Pueblo IV 1300-1450 AD - Character of pottery changed, influence of Mexico pottery, more figurines, glazing, each area such as Hopi, Salado, Zuni, and Rio Grande produced characteristic types. Very collectable period of pottery.

Pueblo V Historic Period. Decline in pottery with a revival beginning in the 20th century.

Hohokam Culture

Pioneer Period 300 BC-500 AD - Pottery produced in seven types; unpainted, painted, and decorated types, various colors and shapes, some polychrome, some clay human figures, paddle-and-anvil method differed from the Anasazi coil method.

Colonial Period 500-900 AD - Pottery, many decorated types; red-on-buff common, decorated with animal figures, evidence of trade pots with Anasazi and Mogollon-types such as Santa Cruz red-on-buff and Gila Butte red-on-buff.

Sedentary Period 1100-1400 AD - Pottery four types - Gila Plain, Gila Red, Gila Smudged, and familiar Casa Grande Red-on-Buff, made by coiling with paddle and anvil. Two Salado types - Gila polychrome and Tonto polychrome influence of Salado people joining as neighbors during this period.

Mogollon-Mimbres Culture

Pine Lawn Period 400-500 AD - Pottery differs from Anasazi and Hokokam, plain brown or polished red, coiling method.

Georgetown Period 500-700 AD - Pottery San Francisco Red and Alma Plain.

San Francisco Period 700-900 AD - Pottery as above plus Mogollon Red-on-Brown, Three Circle Red-on-White, and Alma Punched.

Three Circle Period 900-1050 AD - Pottery as above plus Mimbres Boldface Black-on-White and Three Circle Neck Corrugated.

Mimbres Period 1050-1200 AD - Pottery San Francisco Red, Alma Plain, and two new types Mimbres Black-on-White and Mimbres Corrugated. Mimbres is very famous for excellent painting and variety of decoration including human, animal, and geometric designs.

Chihuahua Periods 1200-1450 AD - Pottery Salado types, Gila and Tonto polychromes, excellent pottery.

EASTERN NORTH AMERICA
500-900 AD - First pottery

Southern

Plain and decorated bowls made of tempered clay and fiber.

Northern

Granular tempered bowls, possibly introduced from Northeastern Asia.

Southern Area Pottery plain, undecorated, fiber temper, many have been introduced from Central or South America.

Northern Area Pottery probably introduced from northeastern Asia, granular tempered jars, some simple geometric decoration by stamping.

---

[2] This classification is provided as a guide only. It will not be agreed to by all archaeologists and revisions can be made to any classification as more data becomes available for study and review.

[3] Martin, Paul S., George I. Quimby, and Donald Collier. 1947. Indians Before Columbus: Chicago and London: The University of Chicago Press.

Third stage 900-1300 AD - Pottery well developed, painted.

Fourth stage 1300-1700 AD - Pottery best produced in eastern North America, some polychrome, many kinds, some exceptional.

Ohio Area

Burial Mound I Period

Glacial Kame Culture Before 500 AD - pottery possible.

Adena Culture 500-900 AD - Pottery small, grit tempered, unpainted

Burial Mound II Period

Hopewell Culture 900-1300 AD - Pottery common, several types and uses, ceremonial, cooking and "art" types, some decorated, buff or gray.

Intrusive Mound Culture 1100-1400 AD - Undecorated, buff or gray, some painted.

Late Prehistoric Period

Younge Culture 1400-1700 AD - Pottery mostly decorated.

Whittlesey Culture 1400-1650 AD - Pottery tempered with grit or shell, bluish gray to light brown.

Middle Mississippi Culture 1400-1700 AD - Pottery painted and unpainted, abundant.

Fort Ancient Culture 1400-1650 AD - Pottery tan, gray, black, brown; some strap handles.

Illinois Area

Baumer Culture 700-1000 AD - Pottery unpainted jars, flat bottoms, some tempered, some designs.

Red Ocher Culture 700-100 AD - Pottery thick, coarse, unpainted, tempered with granite, tan, buff.

Morton Culture 800-1100 AD - Pottery poor, some decoration.

Hopewell Culture of Illinois 900-1300 AD - Pottery Excellent, cooking and burial usages.

Lewis Culture 900-1300 AD - Pottery thin walled, tempered, decorated.

Middle Mississippi Culture of Illinois 1300-1700 AD - Shell tempered, pottery of many styles, abundant.

Tampico Culture 1300-1700 AD - Pottery heavy, tempered, notched lips, decorated.

Wisconsin-Minnesota Area 700-1700 AD - Pottery unpainted, tempered, decorated, dark gray.

Pacific Slope

California Area Pottery mostly in desert region. In late prehistoric times pottery also was manufactured in southern California and San Joaquin Valley - baskets more commonly used.

Plateau Area No pottery reported.

Northwestern Eskimo Area No pottery.

Southwestern Eskimo Area Some modeled pottery with thick sides, crude, undecorated, unfired and baked, some tempered with volcanic rock.

Prehistoric Pottery of New England

Discoveries of colorful prehistoric pottery in the Southwest by archaeologists during the end of the 19th Century and continuing to the present, have overshadowed interest in prehistoric ceramics found in the New England States.

Prehistoric New England pottery presents a developmental sequence beginning about 300 A.D. and continuing to historic times. Archaeologists have classified the ceramic sequence into four Stages. For those interested in ceramics of New England, an excellent discussion is presented by W.S. Fowler (Fowler 1966) which includes a summation of each pottery stage as follows:

STAGE 1 - Earliest - A.D. 300

1. Shape - conoidal with prominent pointed base.
2. Neck - irregularly straight.
3. Rim - usually rounded.
4. Ware - relatively thick.
5. Construction - coiled with coils often weakly jointed together.
6. Surface - cord-marked inside and outside
7. No decoration - 2 exceptions with cord-marked interiors and exteriors noted at end of period: 1) elemental incised marks, 2) dentate single linear.
8. Temper- coarse mineral (crushed quartz).

STAGE 2 - Intermediate - A.D. 1000

1. Shape - conoidal with a more or less pointed base; sharply undercut at times - rare.
2. Neck - either straight, or somewhat constricted.
3. Rim - usually flat, infrequently rounded, everted lip sometimes both inward and outward, often with simple scored decoration on top and outside of edge.
4. Ware - thick or thin, as may have been required.
5. Construction - coiled, with improved joining of coils.

6. Surface - stick-wiped, or finger or tool-smoothed inside; often cord-marked outside, slightly stick-wiped at times.
7. Decoration on neck - simple motifs; techniques include; punctate, thumbnail jabs, dentate, trailing, push-and-pull, rocker-stamp, and cord-wrapped-stick; infrequently, no decoration.
8. Temper - medium mineral, or shell.

STAGE 3 · Late Prehistoric · A.D. 1400

1. Shape - modified conoidal, pointed base tends to be somewhat rounded.
2. Neck - constricted, sometimes straight, surmounted at times by a narrow collar, usually laminated.
3. Rim - flat and evenly constructed; everted lip, occasionally; often scored decoration appears outside, and sometimes inside as well; top of rim, at times, is bisected all around by same marking tool as used for rest of the design work.
4. Ware - various thicknesses; has improved tensile strength.
5. Construction - coiled, with improved joining of coils
6. Surface - tool-smoothed, or stick-wiped inside; smooth, or cord-marked often partially smoothed, over outside.
7. Decoration on neck and collar - elaboration of design motifs include: cross-hatch, closed in herringbone, plated, chevrons, diamonds, rectangles, and large V's; techniques embrace: incision, dentate, cord-wrapped-stick, and punctate in combination - rare.
8. Temper - fine mineral or shell; vegetable - infrequent.

STAGE 4 · Historic · A.D. 1600

1. Shape - semi-globular, slightly suggestive of the conoidal shape, rarely full globular except for small pots.
2. Neck - decidedly constricted; surmounted by a pressed-out collar, usually but not always with castellations; simple shapes resembling colonial metal kettles without collar and castellations noted during creative decline at end of period, 1650-1675.
3. Rim - usually flat without decorations, sometimes rounded with simple scoring.
4. Ware - thinned with good tensile strength.
5. Construction - no coiling in evidence.
6. Surface - tool-smoothed inside; tool-smoothed, or cord-marked smoothed-over outside.
7. Decoration - on collar, often slightly on neck; chevron variations with multiple linear fill-ins,

occasionally with face or corn bosses added - rare; techniques include incised and line-dentate markings.
8. Temper - fine mineral, or shell; vegetable infrequent.

Historic Pottery. Historic pottery, chronologically, is pottery produced after the arrival of Coronado to the area of New Mexico in 1540. Some define historic pottery as that produced after 1600 A.D. while others use 1700 A.D.

Pottery was produced by many of the Pueblos during the early part of the period, at the Pueblos of Acoma, Pecos, San Felipe, Hopi Villages, Cochiti, Isleta, Jemez, Laguna, Nambe, Picuris, Sandia, San Ildefonso, San Juan, Santa Ana, Pojoaque, Santo Domingo, Zia, Taos, Tesuque, and Zuni. Pottery from this period reflects the most advanced of all pottery produced in North America. There were great varieties of types, styles (Fig. 17), decoration, colors and designs. These, and the contemporary expressions which are an extension of the Historic period, provide the most aesthetically appealing pottery in North America.

By 1900 AD pottery seemed destined to extinction. Except for ceremonial and very limited utilitarian use, native pottery was not in general use or needed by the Indian. The reason was the readily availability of cooking and eating ware from the Anglo culture.

The 20th century has seen a dramatic revival of pottery and the emergence of new types and styles. Thanks to the efforts and encouragement of Federal programs, state and local institutions, traders, museums, anthropologists, and numerous individuals, pottery continues and even flourishes in parts of the Southwest.

Modern or Contemporary. Traditional or modification of traditional-type pottery is being produced by several Pueblos and tribes (Fig 18). Some groups have revived the art of pottery production within the past decade while others have an uninterrupted history of producing fine examples of traditional types. Table 2 provides a current status of traditional pottery-producing Pueblos and tribes. This information was derived primarily from a survey of shops, museums, exhibits, catalogs and through conversations with specialists, traders, dealers, and potters.

Interpretation of designs on contemporary Pueblo pottery is primarily for the benefit of the consumer. The latter requests symbolism and the potter responds. If there is a spiritual meaning within the design I do not think the potter will share this with a non-member. But in conceiving their designs, potters are influenced by tradition, natural elements and events, and by their own creativity.

		RELATIVE LEVEL OF PRODUCTION			
Pueblo/Tribe	**Location**	**Major**	**Moderate**	**Minor**	**Remarks**
Acoma	New Mexico	x			
Cochiti	New Mexico		x		
Hopi	Arizona		x		
Isleta	New Mexico			x	Mostly non-traditional
Jemez	New Mexico		x		
Laguna	New Mexico			x	
Nambe	New Mexico			x	
Pecos	New Mexico			x	Pecos Pueblo V Glaze pottery is being produced by Jemez potters
Picuris	New Mexico			x	
Pojoaque	New Mexico			x	
Sandia	New Mexico			?	If pottery is produced very minor
San Ildefonso	New Mexico	x			
San Juan	New Mexico		x		
San Felipe	New Mexico			x	
Santa Ana	New Mexico			x	No pottery is produced at the pueblo
Santa Clara	New Mexico	x			**Most prolific pottery producer of the Rio Grande pueblos**
Santo Domingo	New Mexico			x	
Taos	New Mexico			x	
Tesuque	New Mexico			x	
Ysleta Tigua	Texas			x	Traditional styles made by modern techniques
Zia	New Mexico		x		
Zuni	New Mexico			x	
Maricopa	Arizona			x	
Mojave	Arizona			x	
Navajo	New Mexico & Arizona		x		
Papago	Arizona			x	
Coushatta	Louisiana			x	
Catawba	Oklahoma & South Carolina			x	
Cherokee	Oklahoma & North Carolina			x	
Pamunkey	Virginia			x	

Table 2 - Current production of traditional and modification of traditional pottery types by Pueblos and tribes of North America, 1980.

Symbolism, defined as designs which have religious or other ceremonial significance, is not seen on marketed Indian (trade ware) pottery. Whether the authentic ceremonial bowl[4] is made and used today is somewhat problematical as it is probably not seen by the non-Indian and, thus, falls outside the scope of this book.

There are "ceremonial type" bowls marketed by several Pueblos but let it suffice to say that these are made for marketing and not for ceremonial use.

EASTERN UNITED STATES

Traditional pottery is being produced by a few tribal groups located East of the Mississippi River. These include the Cherokee, Catawba, Pamunkey, and Choushatta Tribes and possibly by others.

Since 1970 there has been an emerging interest in the ceramic arts both by Native Americans and by collectors. While in the western United States, the pottery tradition has been continuous, it had nearly ceased in the East.

Around the turn of the century pottery production had degenerated or had ceased being made by several tribes.

M.R. Harrington published a paper (Harrington 1908) in which he commented on the state of pottery production by eastern tribes around the turn of the century which is a reasonably short summation:

"Survivals of native ceramic art among the tribes east of the Mississippi are now very rare. It has been long abandoned by the Iroquois, and the northern tribes generally, although a few of the mixed-bloods on Martha's Vineyard, Massachusetts, make a so called "Indian pottery" for the tourist trade, from the gaudy-colored clays of Gay Head; but this is manufactured on a potter's wheel and can hardly be called a survival of the old native art. Moreover, I was informed, much of the ware sold as "Gay Head Indian pottery" is made by white men. The Pamunkey Indians of Virginia—a mixed-blood tribe remnant—still make a few earthen pipes, some of which are of old form, and all of which, I understand, are made by old-time methods to a great degree. The few vessels manufactured now by the Pamunkey for curio hunters are plainly crude attempts to resuscitate the art practised by the grandmothers of the present generation, who made and sold large quantities of ware for domestic use to their white and negro neighbors. This older pottery, judging from the single specimen I collected for Mr. Heye, and others which I have seen, were tempered and shaped by native methods but the forms are evidently of mixed of European origin. The Seminole of Florida remember pottery, but I found no specimens among them. "Old pot, Indian got 'um long time ago, no good too much. Fall littly bit, break 'um." Such was old Crop-ear Charley's explanation, when I inquired why pottery was no longer made. No pottery was found among the Chitimacha of Louisiana, the last piece having been broken within ten or fifteen years; but among the Koasati, also in Louisiana, I found two excellent pieces of old types, although the art is no longer practiced by them. The Choctaw of Mississippi have made no pottery for many years, and, as near as I could discover, the last piece kept by Indians has been broken. The Eastern band of Cherokee in North Carolina still boasts a few old potters, but owing to the lack of demand for their product, the art has been practically abandoned. Cherokee vessels are, or were, made in rather crude and archaic forms, but like Catawba pottery usually differ from most prehistoric vessels in having flat instead of rounded bottoms. Like these prehistoric pottery of the southeastern states the recent Cherokee ware shows decoration applied with a carved paddle". Harrington, (1908 p. 406-407.

The high quality of pottery being produced by the eastern tribes suggests that the art has recovered. Some potters are producing pottery following traditional and modern methods.

---

[4] Several names are used to correctly or incorrectly describe ceremonial pottery such as sacred meal bowl, kiva bowl and prayer bowl. Use of these terms for pottery made for sale seem acceptable if the term suggests a shape or style in lieu of a secretive use.

1. Pitcher, Anasazi, Chaco Canyon style.

2. Cylindrical jar, Anasazi, Chaco Canyon style.

3. Mug, Anasazi, Mesa Verde style.

4. Ladle, Anasazi.

5. Pitcher, Anasazi.

6. Canteen.

7. Seed jar.

8. Vase, Hopi Style.

9. Jar.

10. Jar-bowl transitional form.

11. Bowl, Hopi style.

12. Plate.

13. Bowl, Santo Domingo style.

14. Prayer-meal bowl.

15. Kiva bowl, modern.

16. Bowl, Picuris style.

17. Jar or olla, Hopi style.

18. Water jar, Santo Domingo style.

19. Pitcher, Acoma style.

20. Pitcher, Acoma style.

21. Wedding vase.

22. Jar, Hopi Sikyatki style.

23. Jar, Hopi Sikyatki style.

24. Jar, Zuni and Pecos style.

25. Jar, Historic Zuni style.

26. Jar, vase transitional form, Hopi.

27. Jar, San Ildefonso style.

28. Vase, Maricopa style.

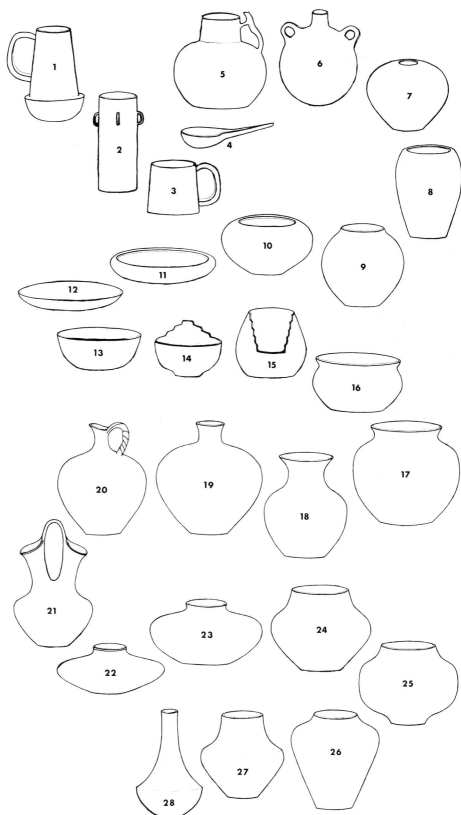

17. Basic styles and shapes of prehistoric, historic, and modern Indian pottery. Drawing by Susan Aizumi.

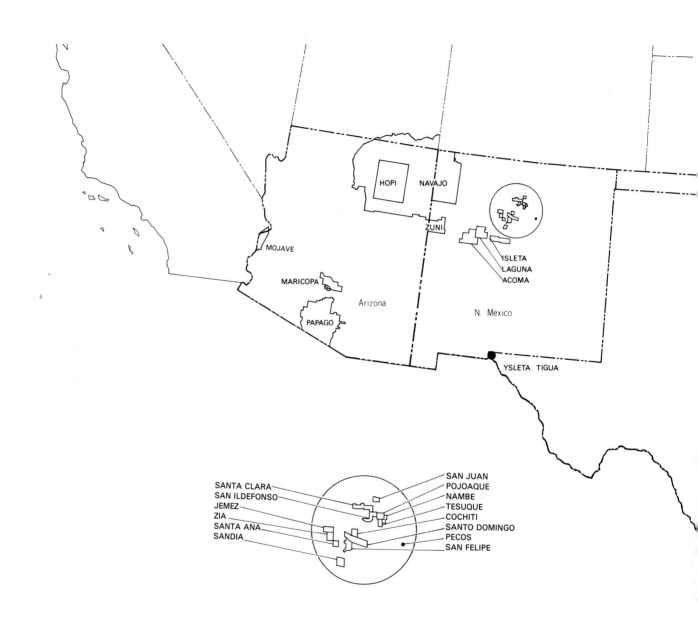

HOPI NAVAJO

ZUNI

MOJAVE

MARICOPA

Arizona

N. Mexico

PAPAGO

ISLETA
LAGUNA
ACOMA

YSLETA TIGUA

SANTA CLARA
SAN ILDEFONSO
JEMEZ
ZIA
SANTA ANA
SANDIA

SAN JUAN
POJOAQUE
NAMBE
TESUQUE
COCHITI
SANTO DOMINGO
PECOS
SAN FELIPE

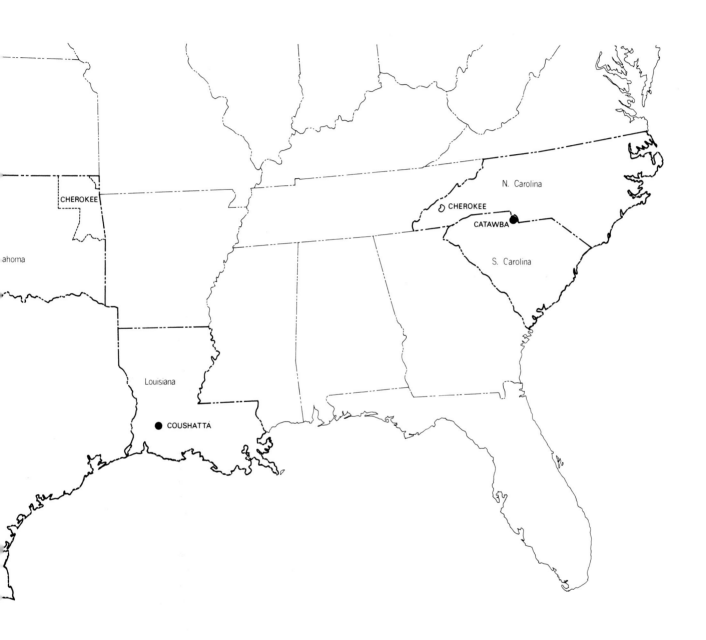

18. Location of Pueblos and tribes producing modern pottery. Drawing by Susan Aizumi.

Federal Sponsorship of Pottery Programs

The Indian Arts and Crafts Board of the U.S. Department of the Interior is a federal agency concerned with the promotion and development of the Native American arts. The Board has encouraged native potters by sponsorship of special exhibits either in Washington, D.C. or at the tribal centers. This has helped to draw attention to the ceramic arts being practiced by some of the eastern tribes. Potters who have exhibited their pottery through the Board's sponsorship in recent years include Elizabeth Bigmeat Jackson, Cherokee; Mabel Bigmeat Swimmer, Cherokee; John and Louise Bigmeat Maney, Cherokee; Cora Wahnetah, Cherokee; Anna B. Mitchell, Cherokee; Mike Daniel, Cherokee, and Georgia Harris, Catawba.

The Institute of American Indian Arts (IAIA), located in Santa Fe, New Mexico, is under the Bureau of Indian Affairs. It is a national institution for training in the arts directed to the special needs of Native Americans. The Institute offers training in painting, graphics, sculpture, ceramics, textiles, dance and writing. Development of the student's creative potential is stressed by encouragement of expression in whatever media the student chooses. Traditional arts are not specifically encouraged or discouraged. Many of today's accomplished Indian artists attended the Institute.

There are numerous alumni of IAIA who have distinguished themselves in the arts. According to Mr. Charles Dailey, Museum Director, the following sampling of IAIA alumni, although not necessarily all inclusive, are setting direction in the broad field of ceramics:

"Laura Gachupin, Jemez; Maxine Gachupin Toya, Jemez; Robert Tenorio, Santa Domingo; Nathan Begaye, Navajo; Manuelita Lovato, Santa Domingo; Otellie Loloma, Hopi; Pete James, Onondaga; Art Cody Haungooah, Kiowa; Darlene James, Hopi; Wilber Bears Heart, Sioux; Peggy Dean Ahvakana, Suquamish; T. A. Sunshine King, Yuchi; Dee Ross, Athabascan; Harold Littlebird, Santo Domingo; Bill Glass, Cherokee; Karita Coffee Wildcat, Comanche; Cyndi Cook, Mohawk; Roberta Tallsalt, Navajo; and Barry Coffin, Pottawatomi. These Indians and others have all come to IAIA with a rich cultural background and much experience in traditional areas and have used the program with its widest possibilities of technology coupling these with intensive training in the study of contemporary ceramics".

"From a new awareness of the wedding between technology, cultural history, philosophy, and the unique relationship with other tribal groups have helped to shape a new and different work of art. Some forms have never been seen or used on a reservation, while others have been only a perfection of traditional shapes and designs used for hundreds of years. No matter what the shape, the cultural imprint and the integrity of the design, the produces and new direction are a direct and original use of the clay emerging from the dust of ten thousand years".

Federally supported programs are encouraging arts and crafts at several reservations. Where there is an interest in ceramics, courses in pottery making may include both traditional and non-traditional methods.

I

THE RAILROAD

Introducing Southwest Pottery Arts

Courtesy Pueblo One

19. Laguna potters trading with tourist, probably at Laguna or Albuquerque, New Mexico, ca 1895-1905. Note the Zia Pueblo sun symbol which is the Santa Fe Railway trademark.

The Railroad
Introducing Southwest Pottery Arts

The railroad which made its debut to the Southwest in 1880 had a significant influence on this territory. By 1885 with the last rail laid and the final spike driven, adventurous travelers from the East could traverse a strange and beautiful country. Those choosing the Southwestern road to California would travel through the colorful mountains and deserts of New Mexico and Arizona territory where militants such as the Apache were struggling their final hours on the last American Frontier. They would see two distinct Indian cultures—one represented by the Apache and the other by the Pueblos. The railroad signaled the beginning of a new era of commerce and social change.

These early travelers, including tourists, anthropologists and archaeologists, represented the first large group to see this land and its people who had inhabited the Rio Grande Valley of New Mexico since the beginning of the 14th Century. The Atchison, Topeka, and Santa Fe Railway even preceeded Adolph F. Bandelier, the father of southwestern archaeology, to the Southwest. Hardships associated with early rail travel did not deter them from discovering the Pueblo culture, customs, adornments, accepting demeanor, and art. Accounts in books, newspapers, and periodicals such as "Harpers Weekly" reflect the interest resulting from this new discovery. The Southwest and the Pueblo people were discovered.

Fortunately for these early railroad passengers, Fred Harvey, an energetic entrepreneur from England convinced Charles Morse, president of the Atchison, Topeka and Santa Fe Railway that hotels and eating establishments were needed along the route to California. The result was the establishment of 100 Harvey Houses at major points through New Mexico, Arizona, and California. Fred Harvey became a legend in the Southwest by providing the highest standard of lodging and meals known in the West. The decor of the Harvey Houses reflected the rich history of the Southwest and the arts of the Pueblos. The "Harvey Girls", impeccable in character and dress were ready to serve the railroad passengers at each of the Fred Harvey Houses. They too have become another legend of the West. When the financial situation threatened completion of the famous La Fonda Hotel in Santa Fe, it was Fred Harvey who came to its aid. Today only one establishment—the restaurant at the Albuquerque airport—retains the Fred Harvey name. But his legend and that of the "Harvey Girls" are inscribed in the archives of western travel.

Herman Schweizer, one of the Fred Harvey's managers, was the first to sell Indian pottery and other arts and crafts at the Coolidge, Arizona, Harvey House. The success of sales resulted in similar merchandise being offered at the other houses. Indian artists and craftsmen were encouraged to demonstrate their techniques and sell their wares at station platforms and Harvey Houses. An illustration of this early marketing method is shown in Fig. 19. Items collected by Schweizer would become the foundation of the famous Fred Harvey Collection. The Easterners had been introduced to a new culture and, therefore, wanted a momento which represented the beauty and culture of the great Southwest and its people. Frequently pottery met the tourist's requirements.

The Atchison, Topeka and Santa Fe Railway spent a reported quarter of a million dollars to promote southwestern tourism for an exhibit at the 1915 World's Fair in San Diego. A pueblo apartment, modeled after Taos Pueblo, and referred to as "The Painted Desert" was constructed, complete with Pueblo potters demonstrating the techniques of pottery manufacture. A 1915 photograph of "The Painted Desert" is shown in Fig. 20.

This is the beginning of the modern era of Indian pottery and the beginning of an awareness which is evident today, thanks in part to the Atchison, Topeka and Santa Fe Railway, to Fred Harvey and to Herman Schweizer.

Unfortunately the tourist demand for pottery had a negative impact. The Indian potter, who was under pressure to produce low priced pots, caused a general decline in quality of traditional pottery. It may not be fair to blame the tourist, as many other factors were at play including governmental policies and disruption of Pueblo culture which had its origin predating the railroad and the tourist. The tourist on the other hand indirectly promoted pottery art by bringing it to the attention of others. Today's popularity and success of this art form may have resulted in part from early tourism to the Southwest.

The advertisements (Figs. 21-24), which were graciously provided by the Santa Fe Railway, illustrates the promotion of railroad travel to the Southwest. It is interesting to note in this advertising material the use of Pueblo pottery symbols to represent the Southwest and its native culture.

World War II signaled the end of railroad tourism to the Southwest. The railroads had introduced Americans to its Southwest, to its native people, and to their ceramics.

This year, 1980, New Mexicans will celebrate a century of railroad travel and freighting.

Courtesy San Diego Museum of Man

20. The Painted Desert Exhibit at the 1915 Panama-California Exposition represents a Pueblo. This was constructed on the edge of San Diego's Balboa Park. (Right) Ramoncita Gonzales (Montoya) sister of Reyita Baros and married to Louis Gonzales. (Left) Alfonsita Pena (Martinez) sister of O. Pena.

21. Atchison, Topeka and Santa Fe Railway advertisement, 1904. Reproduced by their permission.

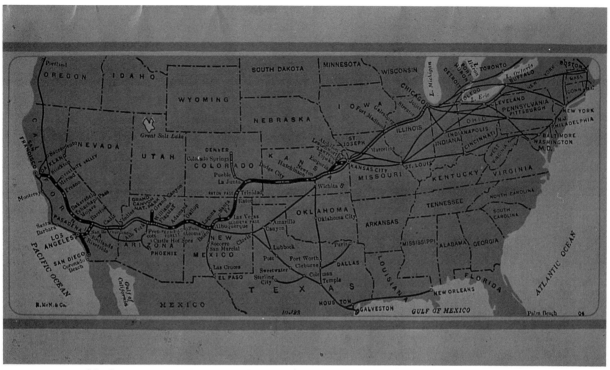

22. Route of the Atchison, Topeka, and Santa Fe Railway system through the Southwest. Reproduced by permission of the Atchison, Topeka, and Santa Fe Railway Company from their 1924 passenger schedule and reproduced with their permission.

23. Cover, Atchison, Topeka, and Santa Fe Railway 1924 passenger schedule of The California Limited and reproduced with their permission.

24. Advertisement from the 1924 passenger schedule of The California Limited and reproduced with their permission.

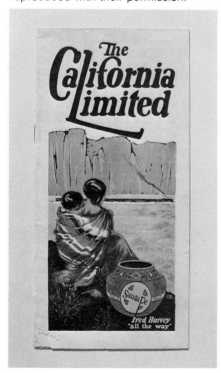

There are Indian pueblos of adobe, all the way from Taos, in sunny New Mexico, out to where the seven Hopi villages are perched on their high mesas. Here a gentle brown race go their rustic ways, much as did their forbears in the days before the Spanish conquistadores.

Canyons de Chelly and del Muerto are in the country of the nomadic Navajos, reached from Gallup, near the eastern Arizona border. These deep clefts in a desert crust point the way to Rainbow Bridge—one of the many wonders off the beaten path in this off-the-beaten-path land.

Lovely Yosemite, and the parks of the California big trees, are at the western end of the long overland journey.

Many of the old Spanish missions of California have been restored and are in an excellent state of preservation. A few are today crumbling ruins.

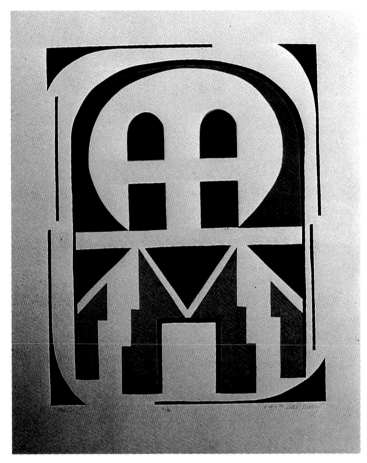

"Blue Corn" Silkscreen by Sandee Barry, 1979.

II

PUEBLOS
of the
SOUTHWEST

Oil ''Noon Visit to the River'' by John Garcia, 1979, Santa
Clara Pueblo. Courtesy Indian Jewelry Center.

PUEBLOS OF THE SOUTHWEST

The Pueblos of the Southwest are a unique group comprising of nineteen individual villages in New Mexico, and one each in Arizona and Texas. The majority of Pueblos live near the center of the Pueblo or in nearby villages. They speak four distinct Indian languages with several dialects (Table 3). Most are bilingual speaking—both their traditional native language and English. Additionally, several speak Spanish. Children from the more traditional Pueblos will speak only their native language until preschool.

The ancestral roots of the modern day Pueblos lead to the "apartment house" ruins scattered throughout the Four Corners area of Utah, Colorado, New Mexico, and Arizona. Known as Anasazi or cliff dwellers, their ancesters were peaceful farmers who abandoned the area during the 13th Century and established numerous Pueblo villages along the Rio Grande River of New Mexico. Archaeologists do not agree on the reason for the southward migration. Internal strife, increased hostile activity, depletion of the soil, drought from 1275 to 1300 AD, or a combination of factors caused the abandoment of the Four Corners area. By 1300 AD the exodus had been completed.

Most Pueblos villages are built around a central plaza or commons which contains one or more kivas. Dances (Fig. 26) are held in the plaza. A Catholic church will be located somewhere in the vicinity of the plaza. The oldest adobe residences will be near the central portion of the Pueblo with newer construction and detached single unit dwellings circling the original area. Some Pueblos still have structures dating back to the 13th Century.

The Pueblo are a proud people who love their village and their land—its rivers, mountains, mesas, and sky. They are the country's best dry-land farmers producing corn, beans, squash, melons, and peppers.

Communical ceremonies, of both prehistoric and historic origins, are ritually practiced in a serious manner by members of the village. There is a dance related to each major event which includes hunting, planting, crop growth, and harvest. Dances begin early in the morning and continue to late afternoon. These are exciting events to participants and observers alike.

Some Pueblos are considered conservative or traditional in adhering to the "old ways" while others have lost most of their customs. Santo Domingo would be an example of the former while Sandia would be an example of the latter. But regardless of their degree of conservatism, the Pueblos have a deep sensitivity to pottery. Their sensitivity is undescribeable but very perceivable. There is nothing comparable for an analogy in the Anglo-society.

Each Pueblo has its own customs and social practices. Seldom are differences among the Pueblos recognized by outsiders. Even a Pueblo from another village may know little about social organization and practices of other Pueblos. And, then, there are clans

Table 3. Cultural organization and language divisions of Pueblos (after Underhill 1954.).

1. UTO-AZTECAN	Hopi (First Mesa)
	Walpi
	Sichomovi
	Hano (Tewa language)
	Polacca
	Hopi (Second Mesa)
	Mishongnovi
	Sipaulovi
	Shungopovi
	Toreva
	Hopi (Third Mesa)
	Oraibi
	New Oraibi
	Hotevilla
	Bacabi
2. KERESAN	Acoma
	Laguna
	Zia
	Santa Ana
	San Felipe
	Santo Domingo
	Cochiti
3. TANOAN	Towa
	Jemez
	Pecos (Decendents at Jemez)
	Tewa
	Tesuque
	Pojoaque
	Nambe
	Santa Clara
	San Ildefonso
	San Juan
	Tiwa
	Taos
	Picuris
	Sandia
	Isleta
	Ysleta
4. ZUNIAN	Zuni

and societies within a Pueblo with practices known only to its members. Pueblos, as an entity and as an individual village, have complex social systems unknown to outsiders. They have kept their secrets and in doing so, they have maintained a social order traceable to before the time of Christ.

The Pueblo people produce a variety of traditional and contemporary arts and crafts: moccasins, woven sash belts, drums, kachinas, jewelry, baskets, sculptures, painting, carvings, and pottery (Table 4 page 200) are examples of their arts and crafts. There

are craftsmen at each Pueblo who produce at least one of these items while the Hopi are pursuing all categories of arts and crafts. They are best known however, for pottery, kachinas, and jewelry.

The Pueblo artists enjoy recognition for artistic achievements but they shun publicity. Art is practiced to satisfy an inner need, not for public acclaim. Perhaps their artistic pursuits have a common basis with their cliff dweller ancestors who created decorative pottery and drew elaborate murals inside kiva walls.

25. "Pueblo Potter" by John Garcia, Santa Clara Pueblo artist.

26. Santa Clara Pueblo "Deer Dance" by John Garcia. Courtesy John Garcia.

III

ARCHAEOLOGY
A New Era

ARCHAEOLOGY—A NEW ERA

Archaeology is entering a new era of public involvement in the United States. The excitement of archaeology—its people, its culture, and its artifacts—is being pursued by an increasing number of people. Concurrently, an era of cooperation is evolving between the professional archaeologist, curators of archaeological sites and museums, and Federal, State and local government, and citizen groups wishing to share the aesthetics and knowledge of prehistoric Americans. Public awareness through educational and interpretive programs is basic to insuring that these resources are adequately managed and protected from abuse and destruction. Areas of archaeological significance are receiving increased attention from the public. Visitors to such sites have increased significantly in recent years.

In response to this growing public interest, direction has been given to Federal land managers to allocate personnel and funds to insure that these cultural resources are identified, evaluated, protected, and managed for the benefit of the public. Chief authority for this drive comes from the National Preservation Act of 1966 which directs land managers to consider impacts on cultural resources resulting from any activity on the land. But concern for cultural resource protection dates to 1906 when

Congress passed an act to provide for the protection of American antiquities on Federal lands. Inadequacies of the law and its enforcement resulted in continual abuse and destruction of many cultural resources, prompting Congress to enact the Archaeological Resources Protection Act of 1979. This new Act provides for archaeological resource protection on Federal and Indian lands. The many provisions of the Act are significant, providing stiff penalties to discourage the destruction, removal, and trade of prehistoric artifacts obtained from these sites. But destruction and vandalism at archaeological sites throughout the United States, resulting in the loss of valuable knowledge, continues to be a major problem of concern to the Federal land manager. Even more serious, however, has been the destruction of entire sites by a few people seeking prehistoric pottery and other artifacts. Numerous incidents have come to light where people have used bulldozers on Federal lands to obtain prized artifacts. The investment of time and equipment, and the willingness to risk detection, reflect the seriousness of this plunder. The greatest loss is the knowledge of past cultures and destruction of a resource which others no longer can enjoy. The resource manager has a considerable management responsibility and

Prehistoric pottery restoration by archaeologist Barbara Peckham, National Park Service, working on pottery sherds from Gran Quivera National Monument. Photo courtesy National Park Service.

challenge even within the limitations of personnel and budgets. In addition to protecting the sites, he must develop and maintain programs involving interpretation, inventory, evaluation, and mitigation of impacts in managing the resource for the benefit of the public. Cooperation of the public is essential to meeting these goals and programs.

The National Park Service was established by an Act of Congress on August 25, 1916, "to promote and regulate the use of the Federal areas known as national parks, monuments, and reservations . . . to conserve the scenery and the natural and historic objects . . . ." Visitors to areas administered by the National Park Service are familiar with the outstanding job performed by this small group of dedicated public servants in managing national parks, monuments, historical sites, and recreation areas. Some of the more popular Park Service archaeological sites with outstanding exhibits of pottery include Mesa Verde, Chaco Canyon, Canyon de Chelly, Bandelier, Fort Ancient, and Russell Cave.

Increasingly, other Federal agencies such as the U.S. Army Corps of Engineers, the Water and Power Resources Service (formerly the Bureau of Reclamation), the Bureau of Land Management, and the USDA Forest Service are implementing plans to inventory, develop, interpret, and protect archaeological resources. In addition to the specific cultural resource laws, archaeological site preservation is included in other environmental acts such as the National Environmental Protection Act, and the National Forest Managment Act.

The USDA Forest Service, which administers 187 million acres of national forests and range lands, has the responsibility of managing numerous prehistoric sites of significant importance. For example, archaeologists from the Pacific Northwest Region of the Forest Service have estimated that there are approximately 40,000 prehistoric sites in that region, which includes the states of Oregon and Washington. Under the National Forest Protection Act, these sites are protected by the Forest Service from potential impact. In addition, through the multiple-use concept, all resources on lands administered by the Forest Service are to be managed for public use, education, and enjoyment. Recreation has developed into a major activity on national forests and it is the intent of the Forest Service to protect, develop, and provide interpretive programs.

Dr. Janet Friedman, archaeologist for the U.S. Department of Agriculture's Office of Environmental Quality, states that "the Department is dedicated to archaeology by law and by policy". An example of this dedication is the "living archaeology concept" currently being developed at Chavez Pass on the Cococino National Forest, Arizona. Nuvaqueotaka is a pueblo complex with approximately 1000 rooms which was occupied during the 13th and 14th Centuries. These ruins offer a unique recreation experience to interpret prehistoric life and to study archaeological techniques. Pottery from this site is illustrated in Fig. A-F.

According to Forest Service archaeologist Dr. Peter Pilles:

"Under this concept, individuals and family groups would make reservations to live in restored rooms in the ruin itself. Instructed by Hopi Indians, they would learn what prehistoric life was like during 1250-1450 A.D. by performing daily activities using the tools and technology available to the prehistoric inhabitants. This might include pottery making . . . collecting wild plants for food, cooking with pottery vessels, building rooms using natural materials, and rehabilitating a prehistoric agricultural system so that crops could be grown in them once again. In this manner, people can be educated about man's relationships with the natural and social environment. The Forest Service concept of multiple use managment can also be better understood when participants in the program can compare the successes and failures of prehistoric land use with modern concepts of conservation and multiple use management."

Public pursuit of archaeology and cooperation with archaeologists also is developing through various state archaeological societies. Amateurs are participating in field excavations under the direction of a professional archaeologist. Science and the individual benefit from these cooperative ventures. Participants gain first hand knowledge of the culture under investigation while providing manpower which otherwise might not be available. Artifacts are displayed usually by the cooperating institution and are shared with the public. These societies go a long way toward public education and discouraging others from site destruction, while providing an opportunity for the non-professional to pursue his or her interest in archaeology.

With public support and involvement, archaeology is entering a new era of cooperation.

A. Nuvaqueotaka Pueblo Ruins, Arizona. (Left) Bidachochi Polychrome, USNM 157521. (Right) Jeddito Polychrome, USNM 157579. 13th and 14th Century.

B. Nuvaqueotaka Pueblo Ruins, Arizona. (Left) Jeddito Black-on-Yellow, USNM 157546. (Right) Same, USNM 157587. 13th and 14th Century.

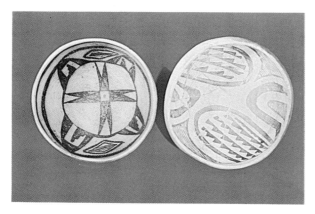

C. Nuvaqueotaka Pueblo Ruins, Arizona. (Left) Awatovi Black-on-Yellow, USNM 157512. (Right) Jeddito Black-on-Yellow, USNM 157610. 13th and 14th Century.

D. Nuvaqueotaka Pueblo Ruins, Arizona. Fourmile Polychrome. 13th and 14th Century. USNM 157524.

E. Nuvaqueotaka Pueblo Ruins, Arizona. 13th and 14th Century. (Left) Homolovi Polychrome, USNM 157589. (Right) Homolovi Polychrome, USNM 157527.

F. Nuvaqueotaka Pueblo Ruins, Arizona. (Left) Bidohochi Black-on-White, USNM 157510. (Right) Jeddito Black-on-White, USNM 157618. 13th and 14th Century.

IV

PRE~HISTORIC
Pottery Section

27

28

27. Prehistoric. Jar, restored. Ontario. J298.

28. Prehistoric. Small pot from burial site at Windsor, Ontario. Wolf Culture. Winterberg Collection. J546.

29

29. Prehistoric. Decorated jar. Pt. Pelee, Ontario. Sanderson Collection, University of Michigan, 1287.

31

30

30. Prehistoric. Large pot from Beecham Site, Ontario. Hauser Collection, Dorchester, Ontario. Courtesy National Museums of Canada #J1395.

31. Prehistoric. Burial pot from Windsor, Ontario site, 1939. Winternberg Collection. J4287.

Fig. 27-31 Courtesy National Museums of Canada

32. Prehistoric. Stage·I, pottery, restored. ca. 300 AD. Massachusetts. (1) Narragansett Bay Site. (2) Wareham. (3) Plymouth. (4) Rimsherds, not to scale, with coarse mineral temper. (5) Assawompsett. (6 & 7) Late State I sherds. Drawings by William S. Fowler. Reproduced by permission of Massachusetts Archaeological Society.

33. Prehistoric. Stage 2 pottery, restored. ca. 1000 AD. Massachusetts. (1,3,7) Narragansett Bay Sites. (2) Duxbury (4&5) Rimsherds, not to scale, with shell or medium mineral temper. (6) Plymouth. Reproduced by permission of Massachusetts Archaeological Society.

34. Prehistoric. Stage 3 pottery, restored. ca. 1000-1400 AD. Massachusetts. (1-2,9) Narragansett Bay Drainage. (10) Kingston, rimsherd profiles, not to scale, with shell or fine mineral temper. (4&5) rimsherds with bisecting of rim tops. (6&7) with laminated collars. (8) with plain flat rim. Reproduced by permission of Massachusetts Archaeological Society.

35. Historic. Stage 4 pottery, restored. ca. 1600 AD. (Upper left & Upper right). Cape Cod. (Center and Lower left) Narragansett Bay Drainage. (Upper right) Cape Cod. Reproduced by permission of Massachusetts Archaeological Society.

32

33

34

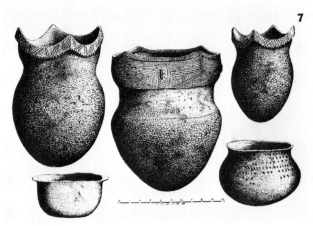

35

Fig. 32-35 Drawings by William Fowler.

36

36. Historic. Pot probably Stage 4 (ca 1600 AD). from New England area. Courtesy National Museum of Canada 20087.

37

37. Historic. Iroquois pottery, restored, ca 1600 AD. Upper Delaware River Valley. Drawing by William Fowler. Reproduced by permission of Massachusetts Archaeological Society.

38

38. Historic. Possibly Iroquois, ca. 1600 AD. Found with skeleton in refuse heap, Rosebuck Village site, Augusta Township, Grenville Co. Courtesy National Museums of Canada 22563.

MIDWEST

39. Prehistoric. Early Woodland, 500-150 BC. Green Lake Co., Wisconsin. d 30.4 cm., h 35.9cm. Courtesy Milwaukee Public Museum A-611-6-1.

40

40. Prehistoric. Hopewell - Esch-Mound (northern Ohio near Lake Erie), ca 100-400 AD. Incised, ca 11.8cm high and 12.2cm wide.

41

42

41. Prehistoric. Hopewell - Mound City (from Mica grave), ca 100 BC. -200 AD. Simple stamped and has punctates, tetrapodal (footed), 11.8cm high and 12.2cm wide, sand tempered.

42. Prehistoric. Duck Pot-Hopewell-Mound (present location and where it was found) ca 100 BC. - 200 AD. Incised, unique, grit tempered, ca 12cm high.

Fig. 40-42 Courtesy Ohio Historical Society

56

43

43. Prehistoric. Hope-well, 200 BC. to 400 AD. Schwert Mound Group, Tempealeau Co., Wisconsin. d 17cm. h 15.5 cm. Courtesy Milwaukee Public Musuem 7844B.

44　　　　　　　　　45

44. Prehistoric. Plains Woodland pot, ca 1 to 1000 AD. Plains Woodland Site Valley Co., Nebraska. Courtesy Nebraska State Historical Society 25VYI-Lab 3.

45. Prehistoric. Middle Woodland. Clear Lake Site (11T^{V}1), Illinois. Courtesy Illinois State Museum 1250.

46

46. Prehistoric. Hope-well (Middle Woodland). Steuben Site (11Ma°202), Illinois. h 7.5cm. Courtesy Illinois State Museum AR 759.

47

48

47. Prehistoric. Hope-
well (Middle Woodland).
Steuben Site (11Ma°202),
Illinois. h 4½″. AR 835.

48. Prehistoric.
400-1000 AD. Nitschke
Mounds, Mound 52, Dodge
Co., Wisconsin. Courtesy
Milwaukee Public Museum
401861.

49

50

49. Prehistoric. Late
Woodland. Gracey
Mounds (11Mp°4), Illinois.
AR 899.

50. Prehistoric. Middle-
Late Woodland. Weaver
Site (11F^{V}229), Illinois. h
36.45cm. AR 1570.

51

51. Prehistoric. Late
Woodland. Weaver Site
(11F^{V}220), Illinois. (Left)
39.9cm. (Right) 13.05cm.
AR 1575

Fig. 47, 49-51 Courtesy Illinois State Museum

52

53

54

55

52. Prehistoric. Late Woodland. Weaver Site (11F^{V}229), Illinois. H 35.4cm. Courtesy Illinois State Museum AR 1569.

53. Prehistoric. Gourd shape ceramic vessel. Middle Mississippian, ca 1050-1200 AD. Aztalan, Jefferson Co., Wisconsin. d 13.6 cm. 1 24.0 cm. Courtesy Milwaukee Public Museum 70119.

54. Prehistoric. Pot, ca 1000-1450 AD. Central Plains Tradition, village site in Nemaha Co., SE Nebraska. Courtesy Nebraska State Historical Society 25NH3-Lab 2.

55. Prehistoric. Fort Ancient, Anderson Component, Anderson site, ca 1200 AD. Incised w/ gillouche, cord-marked, strap handles. Courtesy Ohio Historical Society.

56

57

56. Prehistoric. Fort Ancient-Madisonville component, ca 1400-1600 AD. Cord-marked, strap handles (broken off), shell tempered. Courtesy Ohio Historical Society.

57. Prehistoric. Fort Ancient-Madisonville component, ca 1400-1600 AD. from Indiana. Shell tempered, height 47.7cm.

58

58. Prehistoric. Fort Ancient-Madisonville component(?), ca 1400-1600 AD. Appears to be plain.

59

59. Prehistoric. Upper Mississippian (Oneota), ca 800-1600 AD. Karow Campsite, Winnebago Co., Wisconsin. d 13.5cm., h 9.8cm. Courtesy Milwaukee Public Museum A-616-A.

Fig. 56-58 Courtesy Ohio State Historical Society

TWO INCHES

61

Fig. 60-62 Courtesy Mike Boyatt.

60. Prehistoric. Hooded human effigy bottle. Dallas Culture 1200 to 1600 AD. d 3″, h 4″. Color-Bell Plain. Bussell Island Site (4OLD17). Loudon Co., Tennessee. Note. The late phase of the Mississippian temple mound age in eastern Tennessee, the Dallas Culture, received its name from the large site that occupied both sides of the Tennessee River at Dallas located a few miles above Chattanooga, Tennessee. The Dallas Culture was the forerunner of the historic Creek Indians.

61. Prehistoric. Carson Red-on-Buff (most of red has disappeared). Mississippian Culture, ca 1400 to 1600 AD. d7″, h 6½″. Found Lauderdale Co., Tennessee. Blake Gahagan comments — The Head pot is a very rare type vessel. Only about 6 have been found in Tennessee.

62. Prehistoric. Engraved black, polished vase. ca 1200 to 1600 AD. Moundville, Alabama. d 6″, h 8″. Swirls engraved after firing.

62

63. Prehistoric. (Left) Small bowl with molded pie crust rim. Mississippian Culture 1200 to 1600 AD. d 3″, h 1½″. Color - Bell Plain. Hiwassee Island Site (40MG31). Meigs Co., Tennessee. (Center) Jar. Mississippian Culture 1200 to 1600 AD. d 4″, h 3¼″ Color Bell Plain. Bussel Island Site (40LD17). Loudon Co., Tennessee. (Right) Cane impressed bowl. Mississippian Culture 1200 to 1600 AD. d 3¼″, h 2¼″. Color - Bell Plain. River cane used to make the design below the rim.

63

64. Prehistoric. Fish effigy bowl. Dallas Culture 1200 to 1600 AD. d 3¾″, H 2″. Color - Bell Plain. Bussel Island Site (40LD17). Loudon Co., Tennessee.

64

65. Prehistoric. Turtle shell effigy bowl. Dallas Culture 1200 to 1600 AD. d 5″, h 2″. Color - Bell Plain. Bussel Island Site (40LD17). Loudon Co., Tennessee.

65

Fig 63-65 Courtesy Blake Gahagan.

66

67

66. Prehistoric. Strap handle pot. Dallas Culture 1200 to 1600 AD. d 5½", h 3½". Color - Bell Plain. Bussel Island Site (40LD17). Loudon Co., Tennessee.

67. Prehistoric. Frog effigy bowl. Dallas Culture 1200 to 1600 AD. d 5½", h 3". Color - Bell Plain. Bussel Island Site (40LD17). Loudon Co., Tennessee.

68

68. Prehistoric. Rattle-head human effigy bowl. Dallas Culture, ca 1200 to 1600 AD. Hafford Farm Site, Anderson Co., Tennessee d 6¾", h 4". Blake Gahagan comments —

The human effigy head on this bowl was made hollow and a small hole was left in the back. The vessel then was fired. Small pebbles were then put inside the hollow head and the hole sealed.

69. Prehistoric. Mississippian Culture. Weaver Site (11F^{V}229), Illinois. h 35.1cm. Courtesy Illinois State Museum AR 1574.

69

Fig. 66-68 Courtesy Blake Gahagan.

63

70. Prehistoric. Mississippian Culture. Weavers Site (11F^V228), Illinois. (Left h 9.9cm (Center h 9.8cm (Right) 9.0cm. AR 1573.

71. Prehistoric. Upper Mississippian. Culture to Early Historic. Zimmerman Site (11Ls^V13), Illinois h 14½ cm. AR 1590

72. Prehistoric. Incised bowl. Caddo 1300-1700 AD d 5¼″, h 3¼″. McCurtain Co., Ok.

73. Prehistoric. Pot, ca 1200-1600 AD. Oneota Village Site, Richardson Co., SE Nebraska. 25 RHI-Lab 25.

74. Prehistoric. Pot, ca 1200 to 1800 AD. Oneota Village Site, Richardson Co., SE Nebraska. 25 RHI-Lab 23.

75. Historic. Pots, Dismal River, ca 1675-1725 AD. Chase Co., SW Nebraska. 25 CHI-Lab 25.

70

Courtesy Illinois State Museum.

71

72

73

75

74

Fig. 73-75 Courtesy Nebraska State Historical Society.

76

77

76. Historic. Pawnee, ca 1750 to 1850. Pawnee Village site, Butler Co., east-central Nebraska. 25 BUI-Lab 1.

77. Historic. Pawnee, ca 1750-1850 AD. Pawnee village site, Nance Co., east-central Nebraska.

Fig. 76-77 Courtesy Nebraska State Historical Society

SOUTHWEST

"Evening Light On the Mesa", oil, 21½″ x 32½″, W.R. Leigh, from the book *W.R. Leigh* by June Du Bois, p. 140.

Courtesy June Du Bois

79

80

81

78. Prehistoric. Basket possibly lined with clay. Westwater Ruin #1777, Utah. Ca. 100 to 500 AD. 571-5, P.1.

79. Prehistoric. Tooled vessel, intrusive into the Pueblo Culture Coombs site. Fremont Culture, ca 400 to 1250 AD. (?) h 10". Glen Canyon Project, University of Utah, Department of Anthropology. 571.5, P.4.

80. Prehistoric. North Creek Fugitive red water jar. Fremont Culture, ca 400 to 1250 AD. (?). Coombs site near Boulder, Utah. h 15". Glen Canyon Project, University of Utah, Department of Anthropology. 571.5, P.3.

81. Prehistoric. Corrugated utility vessel from Coombs site. Fremont Culture, ca 400 to 1250 AD. (?). Glen Canyon Project, University of Utah, Department of Anthropology. 571.5, P.5.

Fig. 78-81 Courtesy Utah Historical Society

82   83

84

85

82. Prehistoric. Mancos Black-on-White water jar, Pueblo II. 900 to 1050 AD. d 12″. Glen Canyon Survey Project, University of Utah, Department of Anthropology. 571.5, P.2.

83. Prehistoric. Possibly Deadmans Black-on-Red. Kayenta, Mesa Verde, or Virgin. Anasazi 275-1066 AD (?). Washington Co., Utah (Left) Bowl. d 9″, H 6″. (Center). Pitcher h 6″. (Right) Bowl d 9¼″, h 5″. Courtesy Spense Esplin.

84. Prehistoric. Pottery in association with burial, ca 1150 AD., typical of those found in Glen Canyon, Utah. Burial is Moqui Canyon and Castle Wash area. Glen Canyon Project, University of Utah, Department of Anthropology. 571.3, P.3.

85. Prehistoric. Tusayan Black-on-White storage jar. 1075 to 1285 AD. Glen Canyon Project, University of Utah, Department of Anthropology. 571.3, P-1.

Fig. 82, 84-85 Courtesy Utah Historical Society

67

86. Prehistoric. Santa Fe Black-on-White bowl, without slip, 13th Century. This is an unusual form. Dug by Frederick C.V. Worman at Los Alamos Site LA4634, Pajarito Plateau, New Mexico. Courtesy Charlie R. Steen and Los Alamos Scientific Lab. 634450.

86

87

87. Prehistoric. Corrugated utility olla, Pueblo III. 1050 - 1300 AD. Indentations or corrugations made by pinching coils as they are built. Mesa Verde National Park. Courtesy N P5, MEVE 70128.

88

88. Prehistoric. Black-on-White. Ladle, restored. Anasazi 1100-1250 AD. L. 10″. Courtesy Pueblo One.

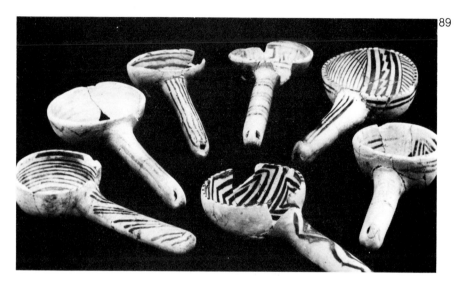

89

89. Mesa Verde Black-on-White, ladles. Pueblo III or Classic Pueblo Period. 1050 to 1300 AD. Mesa Verde National Park. Courtesy National Park Service #71-436-3.

90

90. Prehistoric. Mesa Verde Black-on-White, bowls, mug, and one corrugated utility jar. Pueblo III or Classic Pueblo Period. 1050 to 1300 AD. Pottery from Mesa Verde National Park. Courtesy NPS, 71-436-5.

91. Prehistoric. Rio Grande corrugated olla, utility ware. No exact provenience, Pajarito Plateau, New Mexico. Courtesy Charlie R. Steen.

91

92

92. Prehistoric. Tonto Polychrome olla, restored. Salado 1250-1400 AD. d 14″, h 10¾″. Courtesy Pueblo One.

93

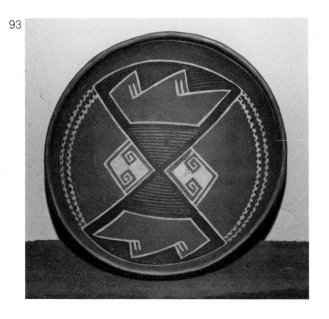

93. Prehistoric. Fourmile Polychrome bowl, restored. White mountains. Anasazi 1325-1400 AD. d 8¾″, h 3¾″. Courtesy Pueblo One.

Fig. 97-99 Courtesy Pueblo One

94. Prehistoric. Tulaosa Black-on-White pitcher. Anasazi 1100 to 1250 A.D. d 6″, h 6″.   **95.** Prehistoric. Salado redware pitcher. Anasazi 1250-1400 A.D. d 6½″, h 5-5/8″.   **96.** Prehistoric. Corrugated utility ware. Anasazi 1000-1400 A.D. (Left d 4″, h 4″. (Right) d 5½″, h 4¼″.   **97.** Prehistoric. Roosevelt Black-on-White jar. Anasazi ca 1200 A.D. d 7″, h 9½″.   **98.** Prehistoric. Roosevelt Black-on-White jar. Anasazi ca 1200 A.D. d 7″, h 9½″.   **99.** Prehistoric. Four Mile Polychrome bowl. Anasazi. 1300-1400 A.D. White Mountain. d 10¾″, h 4½″.

Fig. 100-104 Courtesy Pueblo One

100. Prehistoric. Pinedale Polychrome bowl, restored. Mogollon Rim, Anasazi 1275-1350 A.D. d 10″, h 4½″.　**101.** Prehistoric. Pinedale Polychrome bowl, restored. Mogollon Rim, Anasazi 1275-1350 A.D. d 10¼″, h 4¾″.　**102.** Prehistoric. Pinedale Polychrome bowl, restored. Anasazi 1275-1350 A.D. d 11″, h 5¼″.　**103.** Prehistoric. Mimbres Black-on-White bowl. Mogollon 1100 to 1250 A.D. d 9¾″, h 5½″.　**104.** Prehistoric. Mimbres bowl. Mogollon 1100-1250 A.D. d 9½″, h 4½″.

105

106

109

107

108

Fig. 105-107 Courtesy Pueblo One; 108, 109 Courtesy Marguerite Kernaghan

105. Prehistoric. Tonto Polychrome jar, restored. Anasazi, Salado Branch 1300-1400 A.D. d 15½″, h 10½″. **106.** Prehistoric. Tonto Polychrome jar, restored. Anasazi, Salado Branch, 1300-1400 A.D. d 9½″, h 13½″. **107.** Prehistoric. Tonto Polychrome jar, restored. Anasazi, Salado Branch 1300-1400 A.D. d 13″, h 9¼″. **108.** Prehistoric. Anasazi mugs from near Prewitt, NM. Period unknown, possibly Pueblo II. (Left) d 4″, h 4¼″ with flat bottom. (Center) d 5″, h 6″ base concave. (Right) d 4-1/8″, h 5¼″. **109.** Prehistoric. Reserve Black-on-White pitcher. Anasazi 940-1100 A.D. Four Corners area, N.M. D 7¼″, h 7″.

Fig. 110-115 Courtesy Marguerite Kernaghan

110. Prehistoric. (Left) Mesa Verde Black-on-White mugs. Anasazi Pueblo II. (?) (Left) d 3″, h 3″. (Right) d 3″, h 3½″.   **111.** Prehistoric. Black-on-White effigy on a boot jar. Anasazi Pueblo II. From Tonto Basin near Roosevelt Dam, AZ. d 3″, h 3¼″.   **112.** Prehistoric. Black-on-White bowl. Anasazi Pueblo II. d 7″, h 3½″. Marguerite Kernaghan Collection #2660. Photo by S. Kernaghan.   **113.** Prehistoric. Homolovi Polychrome bowl. Anasazi 1300-1400 A.D. Pinedale ruins near Winslow, AZ. d 8½″, h 3½″.   **114.** Prehistoric. Black-on-White pitcher. Anasazi Pueblo II. ca 900-1050 A.D. d 4¼″, h 3¾″. San Juan Basin.   **115.** Prehistoric. Kayenta Black-on-White pitcher with animal figure as handle. Anasazi Pueblo III 1050-1300 A.D. d 6″.

Fig. 116, 117, 119 Courtesy Marguerite Kernaghan; 120, 121 Courtesy Jemez State Monument, Museum of New Mexico.

116. Prehistoric. Hohokam utility ware. (Left) Storage jar. d 5½″, h 4¼″. (Right) Storage jar with lid, rare, d 5¼″, h 5″.   **117.** Prehistoric. (Left) Mesa Verde. Black-on-White jar. Anasazi Pueblo III Period, 1050-1300 A.D. d 5″, h 4″. (Center) Mesa Verde Black-on-White bowl. Anasazi Pueblo III Period, 1050-1300 A.D. d 7″, h 3″. (Right) Utility ware used for cooking, round bottom. Chaco Canyon area. Pueblo III, ca 1050-1300   **118.** Prehistoric. Chihuahua pottery bowl, Madera Black-on-Red (?). ca 1200-1450 A.D. Northern Mexico, d 7″, h 6″.   **119.** Prehistoric. Jeddito. Black-on-Yellow Jar. 1300-1600 A.D. d 8¼″, h 3¾″. Early Hopi, found on Hopi Reservation.   **120.** Prehistoric. Tradeware olla. From Kuaua. ca 1300 A.D.   **121.** Prehistoric. Jemez Black-on-White, Bird form ceremonial bowl. ca 1400 A.D.

122

123

124

125

126

122. Prehistoric. Jemez Black-on-Gray, Ceremonial bowl. ca 1400 A.D.   **123.** Prehistoric. Kuaua Glaze polychrome. ca 1300 A.D. Rio Grande Valley, New Mexico.   **124.** Prehistoric. Jemez Black-on-Gray. Bowl. ca 1600 A.D. Giusewa Site, Jemez Springs, New Mexico. (Note the two holes each side of the crack. This is a form of mending in which a piece of leather or fiber cord was used to connect the two pieces.)   **125-126.** Prehistoric. Two, Glaze II polychrome bowls plastered together. 15th Century. From Pajarito Plateau. In 1978 Danny Ridlon discovered these cemented pots in White Rock Canyon near Los Alamos, New Mexico. Investigation by X-rays and drilling a small hole revealed presence of feathers bound together by yucca fibers. Charlie Steen, Los Alamos archaeologist reported that same feathers have been identified as scarlet macaw and other feathers found in bowl are possibly from another parrot species. The plastered bowls are the first discovery of lime plaster being used by prehistoric people of the Southwest.   *Fig. 122-124 Courtesy Jemez State Monument, Museum of New Mexico; 125, 126 Courtesy Los Alamos Scientific Laboratory*

V

CONTEMPORARY
and
HISTORIC
Pottery Section

127. ''The Pool At Oraibi'', oil, 22½″ x 28¼″, 1917, W. R. Leigh. Oraibi is a Hopi Village at Third Mesa, Arizona.

HOPI

Hopi include both the original Hopi group and the Hopi-Tewa people. The latter moved to First Mesa (Hano) in 1700 AD and assumed the role of a home guard for the Hopi. Today they still retain a language distinctive from the Hopi and maintain a separate cultural and social order. While the Hopi-Tewa are known to have originated from the Rio Grande area of New Mexico, the origin of the Hopi is subject to a less definitive answer. The most widely accepted hypothesis on their origin suggests the Kayenta branch of the Anasazi culture. Therefore, at the Hopi villages there are two groups distinguished by origin, language and by social and cultural practices. Their villages are situated on Mesas known as First, Second and Third Mesa which they have occupied for at least a thousand years. The Hopi were never conquered by the Spanish or by their Navajo neighbors who surround them on all sides.

Prior to 1900 AD pottery production at Second and Third Mesas ceased (Bartlet 1977).[5] The quality of Hopi pottery regressed during the 1920's and 1930's with emphasis on tourist curios—a pattern also observed during this period at several of the New Mexico Pueblos. Some quality pottery was still being produced during this period but it was overwhelmed in quantity by curio pottery. A technical problem also emerged with their black paint smearing after firing. For whatever the cause, if the problem persists, it is evidence of a decline in quality. The same problem has occurred with some Pueblo pottery produced at Hopi, San Ildefonso and at Jemez. The immediate remedy is to seek advice from an older potter. But occasionally potters have resorted to use of a black commercial ceramic paint as a solution. It is difficult to distinguish vegetal and mineral black paint from black ceramic paints which are available commercially.

Prior to the 1940's, Hopi pottery probably sold for less than twenty dollars, while today some pots sell for a thousand dollars or more.

The modern era of Hopi pottery began at the end of the 19th Century with Nampeyo of Hano and

128. Hopi, First Mesa village of Walpi, south view, ca 1900. A. C. Vroman photo.

Courtesy San Diego Museum of Man

79

her revival of the ancient Sikyatki ware. Sikyatki polychrome was made between 1450 and 1550 AD and is characterized by a short vertical axis relative to its horizontal axis, resulting in a "squat" shape bowl. Nampeyo adopted this shape and created her own designs. Through the acceptance of this style, Nampeyo became as well known as Maria Martinez of San Ildefonso.

Today Hopi potters at First Mesa are producing black-on-red, black-on-white, black and red on white slip, and plain red polish which may be indented. An incised polished pottery depicting both naturalistic and representative designs is being made by Wallace Youvella. His non-traditional style represents a creative specialty from the pottery tradition, similar to that of Joseph Lonewolf of Santa Clara, rather than signaling a new Hopi style. Hopi potters and Hopi pottery buyers are basically traditionalists.

In addition to trade ware, the Hopi still make pottery for their own use—the piki and mush bowl for mixing cornmeal are examples.

Some of the known potters at First Mesa in recent years include those of the Nampeyo family, Garnet Pavatea, Verla Dewakuku, Alma Tahbo, Marcia Fritz, Joy Navasie, Sadie Adams, Mary Ami, Fannie Nampeyo, Lorna Adams, Loma Kemo, Elizabeth White, Violet Huma and Rena Kevena. In 1977 Grace Chapella who was born two years before Custer and the Little Bighorn, was still making pottery.

The pottery tradition at First Mesa is strong and the future looks bright for its continuation and growth.

---

[5] Today there may be limited pottery production for internal use at Second and Third Mesas.

129. Hopi. Sikyatki Polychrome with Germination Kachina design. 15th Century. Private Collection.

130. Hopi. Walpi Polychrome. ca 1795. d 14″, h 9″.

131. Hopi. Wallace Youvella. Red carved bowl, butterfly design. 1979. d 2¾″, h 2½″.

132. Hopi. Frogwoman. ca 1970. d 5½″, h 3″.

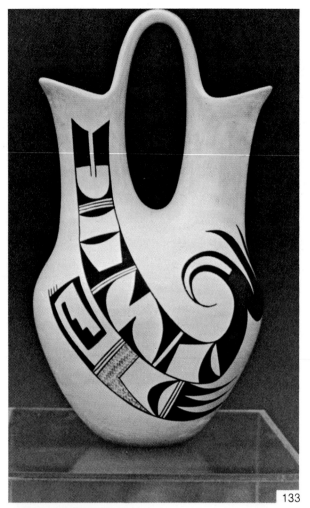

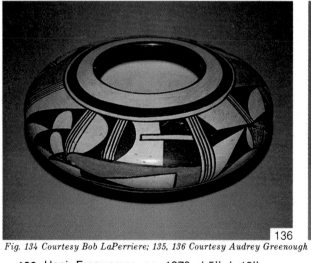

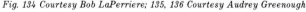

Fig. 134 Courtesy Bob LaPerriere; 135, 136 Courtesy Audrey Greenough

133. Hopi. Frogwoman. ca. 1970. d 5'', h 13''.
135. Frogwoman. Fine bowl. ca. 1930. d 4½'', h 4''
d 7½'', h 5½''.

134. Hopi. James Huma. ca 1970. d 4'', h 3''.
136. Same as Fig. 135. **137.** Hopi.

138

139

140

141

142

Fig. 139 Courtesy Marguerite Kernaghan; 140 Courtesy Audrey Greenough

138. Hopi. Frogwoman. ca 1978. d 4'', h 8''.   **139.** Hopi. Frogwoman. 1978. (Left) d 5¼'', h 6¼''. (Right) d 7¼'', h 8''.   **140.** Hopi. Hano Polychrome, ca 1940. d 4½'', h 8''.   **141.** Hopi. Dextra Nampeyo. 1978. d 5½'', h 3''.   **142.** Hopi. Garnet Paveta. 1978. d 6'', h 5¼''.

Fig. 143, 147 Courtesy Pueblo One; 144 Courtesy Leon Hodge; 145, 146 Courtesy Nancy Daughters

143. Hopi. Fannie Nampeyo. ca. 1940. d 4''.

145. Hopi. Frogwoman. 1975. d 6'', h 4½''.

147. Hopi. Myrtle Young. Dough bowl. 1970. d 13'', h 4''.
1920. d 8″.

144. Hopi. Fannie Nampeyo. ca. 1965. d 3'', h 3''.

146. Hopi. Sadie Adams. 1973. d6'', h3½''.

148. Hopi. Sichornori Polychrome. ca 1929. d 8''.

Fig. 150 Courtesy Pueblo One; 151 Courtesy Gila River Arts & Crafts Center; 153 Courtesy Jerry Mamola

149. Hopi. Bowl has crack on rim. ca. 1910. d 8'', h 5¼''.   **150.** Hopi. Bowl. ca 1950, d 12½'', h 3''.
151. Hopi. Verla Dewakuku. ca 1975. d 10½'', h 4¾''.   **152.** Hopi. Helen Poolheco. 1979. d 5'', h 4''.
153. Hopi. ca. 1930. d 6'', h 5''.   **154.** Hopi. Verla Dewakuku. ca 1970. d 7¾'', h 4⅞''.

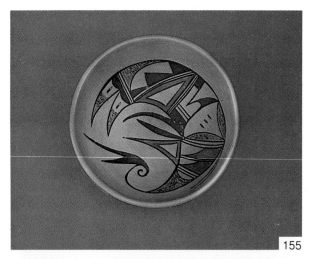

155

156

157

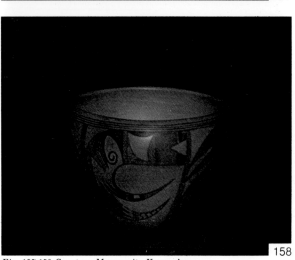

158

159

Fig. 157-159 Courtesy Marguerite Kernaghan

155. Hopi. Vina Harvey. ca 1975. d 7'', h 3¾''.   **156.** Hopi. Ada Yayetwea. ca 1975. d 11¼'', h 4½''.
157. Hopi. (Left) Elva Nampeyo. 1977. d 3¼'' x 4¾''. (Right) Fannie Nampeyo. 1975. d 3½'' x 4½''.
158. Hopi. Rodina Huma. d 7½'', h 6''.   **159.** Hopi. Vina Harvey. 1977. d 5¾'', h 5½''.

Fig. 160 Courtesy Marguerite Kernaghan; 162-165 Courtesy Leon Hodge

160. Hopi. Marsha Ricky. 1975. d 8''h 8''. **161.** Hopi. Marcia Fritz. ca. 1960. d 9¼'' x h 3¼''.
162. Hopi. Marcia Fritz. ca 1977. d 5¾'', h 2⅞''. **163.** Hopi. ca. 1977. d 2¼'', h 1¾''. **164.** Hopi. ca. 1977.
d 5¾'', h 2⅝''. **165.** ca 1977. d 4⅝'', h 2½''.

Fig. 166-170 Courtesy David Ichelson

166. Hopi. Nampeyo. ca 1940. d 6¾'', h 3''.
168. Hopi. Black-on-Red. ca. 1965. d 5½'', h 4''.
170. Hopi. Polychrome. ca 1960. d 4½", h 3½".

167. Hopi. Black-on-Red. ca. 1945. d 5½'', h 4'',
169. Hopi. Polychrome ca. 1960. d 5¼'', h ½''.

ACOMA

The historic Pueblo of Acoma, reported to be the oldest continuously inhabited community in the United States, has a long tradition of producing high-quality pottery. Visitors to Acoma always will find activity on this beautiful Mesa during the tourist season and on weekends. Several potters display their wares on the Mesa. There are few full-time residents at Acoma or "Sky City" as it is sometimes called. The majority of Acoma people live in the near-by communities of Acomita, McCartys, and San Fidel where most Acoma pottery is produced. Many potters make frequent visits to the Mesa or reside there as summer residents.

Technically traditional Acoma pottery is of high quality and is superbly executed. It is thin-walled and strong. Consequently it is sought after by collectors and museums alike.

Acoma pottery is painted with a kaolin clay slip before decorating and firing. The pottery may be plain with a smooth white slip, white with indentations, black-on-white, or white-on-black. The most common are polychromes of orange, black and brown-on-white. Present day designs include deer, birds, flowers and geometric patterns. Fine-lined designs of geometric patterns in black or brown on a white background are made by several Acoma potters. Mimbres and Hohokam inspired styles also are being made by a few potters. Figurines of owls and turtles, and other miniatures are common and directed toward the tourist market. Several potters still make large jars, ollas, and vases which are ideally suited for accent in both traditional and contemporary decor.

There are two problems with some Acoma pottery, one technical and the other philosophical.

Pitting on the slipped surface, which is manifested by small pits one to two mm in diameter, occurs on some pottery. Pitting may result from clay impurities or a failure in preparation of the clay. Unfortunately, the pitting may not develop until some weeks after firing to the chagrin of the owner.

The potter usually can patch the pits but this is seldom a practical approach. The potter shares concern with the consumer and makes every known effort to avoid this problem.

In recent years some Acoma potters have resorted to use of commercial greenware and molds to make inexpensive pottery, particularly small animals. Large wedding vases and bowls made in this manner have been marketed in Albuquerque. The motivation is not deception but rather a desire to produce more pottery to meet the demand. Also the potters may never have learned the traditional method. It is advisable to inspect the pot carefully and ask questions if you have doubts.

Many Acoma potters still refrain from signing their pots in response to a desire for anonymity which is characteristic of the Pueblo cultures. This practice, however, is changing and more pottery is appearing on the market with signatures. It is still common practice to place the words "Acoma-Sky City" on the bottom of pots. Lack of a personal signature does not suggest any less pride on behalf of the potter nor does it indicate inferior quality.

There are several noted Acoma potters. The list might include Lucy Lewis and her daughters, Anne, Emma, Mary and Delores; Mary Z. Chino; Rose Chino Garcia; Grace Chino; Barbara Cerno; Juanita Keene; Stella Shutiva; Joseph M. Cerno; Lillian Salvador; Lolita Concho; Francis Torivio; Wanda Aragon; Delores Sanchez and many others.

Acoma Pueblo, New Mexico, 1979. **171.** Street scene. **172.** Typical Pueblo ladder used to reach upper apartments.

173

174

175

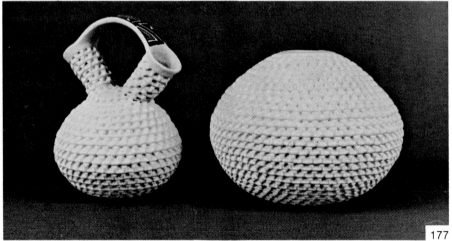

176

177

Fig. 173-175 Courtesy Pueblo One; 176, 177 Courtesy Al Anthony, Adobe Gallery.

173. Acoma. Polychrome olla. Late 19th Century. h 10''. Richard M. Howard Collection.　　**174.** Acoma. Polychrome ollas. (Left) ca. 1870. h 9½''. Collection of Pueblo One. (Center) ca. 1850. h 12''. Collection of Pueblo One. (Right) Late 19th Century. h 9''. Private collection.　　**175.** Acoma. Polychrome olla. late 19th Century. h 11½''. The Collings Collection　　**176.** Acoma. Polychrome olla. ca. 1910.　　**177.** Acoma. Stella Shutiva. (Left) Corrugated wedding vase. 1979. d 6'', h 8''. (Right) Corrugated seed bowl. 1979. d 10'', h 6½''.

Fig. 178, 182 Courtesy Marguerite Kernaghan

178. Acoma. Emma Lewis. Polychrome canteen with Mimbres lizard design. ca. 1975. d 5″.   **179.** Acoma. Mary Lewis. Hump-back flute player design. 1975. d 4½″, h 5″.   **180.** Acoma. Lucy M. Lewis. Deer design. 1977. d 5¾″, h 4″.   **181.** Acoma. Emma Lewis. Mimbres design. 1977. d 2¾″, h 3″.   **182.** Acoma. Lucy M. Lewis. 1975. (Left) d 3½″, h 3½″. (Right) d 3¾″, h 4″.

183

184

185

186

187

Fig. 186, 187 Courtesy Marguerite Kernaghan

183. Acoma. Lucy M. Lewis. Hump-back flute player design. 1977. d 4¼'', h 3''.   **184.** Acoma. Emma Lewis. Polychrome bird design. 1977. d 2⅜'', h 1¾''.   **185.** Acoma. Emma Lewis. Deer-heart design. 1977. d 4¼'', h 3⅜''.   **186.** Acoma. Marie Z. Chino. Polychrome wedding vase. ca. 1970. d 12½'', h 8½''.   **187.** Acoma. Juanita Keene. Polychrome. ca. 1977. d 8¼'', h 6½''.

190

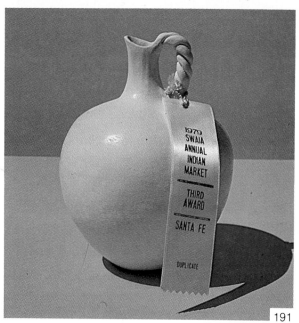

191

Fig. 188-190 Courtesy Marguerite Kernaghan

1889. Acoma. Polychrome. ca. 1920. d 6'', h 8''.
189. Acoma. Polychrome vase. ca 1940. d 8¾'', h
10¾''.   **190.** Acoma. Polychrome canteen. ca.
1930. d 9''.   **191.** Acoma. Junita Keene. Semi-matte
white pitcher, award winner at 1979 Santa Fe Indian
Market. 1979. d 7½'', h 9''.

192. Acoma. Marie Z. Chino. Polychrome jar. ca 1950. d 8'', h 6½''.   **193.** Acoma. Ethel Shields. Polychrome jar. ca. 1960. d 9½'', h 9''.   **194.** Acoma. Polychrome jar. ca. 1950. d 7'', h 5½''.   **195.** Acoma. (Left) Polychrome jar. ca. 1950. d 7½'', h 5''. (Right) Polychrome wedding vase. ca. 1950. h 7¾''.   **196.** Acoma. Fine design. ca 1950. d 4'', h 3½''.   **197.** Acoma. Polychrome jar, poor quality, ca. 1960, d 10½'', h 8½''.

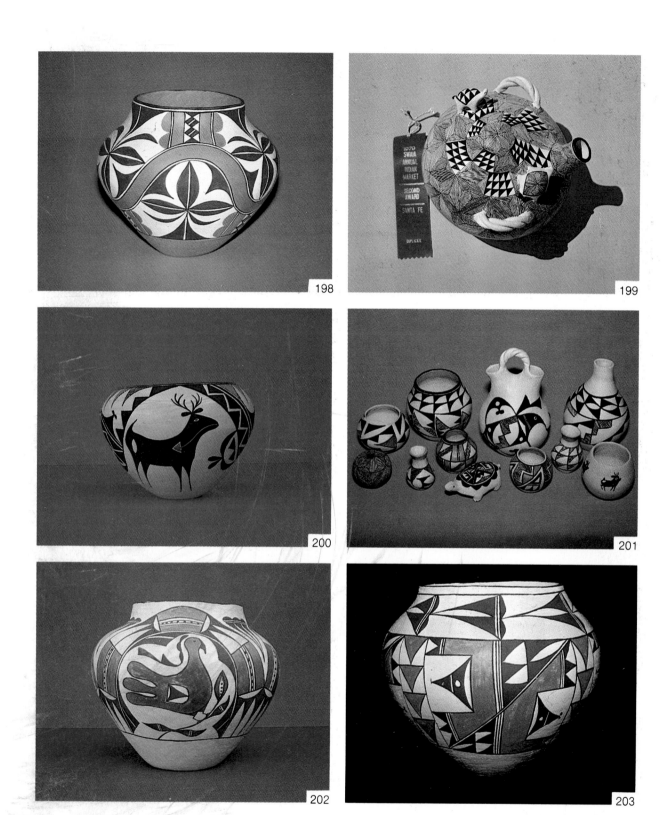

198. Acoma. Juanita Keene. Polychrome olla. 1979. d 10'', h 9''.　　**199.** Acoma. Rose Chino Garcia. Canteen. 1979. d 9'',　h 6½''.

200. Acoma. Sara Garcia. Polychrome olla deer-heart line design. 1977. d 7⅝'', h 5¼''.　　**201.** Acoma. Miniatures. ca 1977.　　**202.** Acoma. Dorris Patricio. Polychrome jar, bird design. 1979. d 11'', h 9''.　　**203.** Acoma. Dorris Patricio. Polychrome jar. 1979. d 9'', h 7¼''.

Fig. 206 Courtesy David Ichelson; 207 Courtesy Marguerite Kernaghan; 208 Courtesy Pueblo One

204. Acoma. (Left) d 4'', h 3¼''. 1979. (Right) M. Chino. 1979. d 3¾'', h 2½''. (Foreground) J. Aragon. 1977. Pendant. d 1⅜''.   **205.** Acoma. (Left) d 3'', h 2''. 1979. (Right) 1979. d 2'', h 1¼''.   **206.** Acoma. Black-on-White. ca 1960. d 6'', h 4½''.   **207.** Acoma. Charmae Shields. Polychrome olla. 1979. d 7½'', h 5¾''.   **208.** Acoma. Historic. Polychrome. 1840-1860. d 12½'', h 11½''.

Fig. 209-211, 213 Courtesy Pueblo One; 212 Courtesy David Ichelson

209. Acoma. Historic. Polychrome, bottom of jar marked "Stevenson Bureau of Ethnology." 1870-1880. d 11", h 9".   **210.** Acoma. Historic. Polychrome. ca 1890. d 10", h 5½".   **211.** Acoma. Jar. ca 1890-1900. d 10½", h 9½".   **212.** Acoma. Polychrome jar. ca 1900-1910. d 11½", h 1½".   **213.** Acoma. Fine Jar, Black-on-White design. ca 1910. d 13", h 11".   **214.** Acoma. Jar with Black-on-White design. ca 1920-1930. d 13", h 11".

LAGUNA

A federally funded program begun in 1973 under the direction of Evelyn Cheromiah, an accomplished Laguna potter, has revived traditional ceramics at Laguna Pueblo.

Laguna pottery is similar in style, design, and color to Acoma wares. The close proximity to a Pueblo with a strong pottery tradition and their common language are offered as an explanation. A specialist is usually required to distinguish Acoma pottery from those of Laguna. Generally, designs on Laguna ware are not as detailed or as well executed as Acoma designs. Harlow (1977) provides an excellent discussion of identifying characteristics for those who wish to review differences as well as similarities between Acoma and Laguna pottery.

U.S. Army Captain John C. Bourke reported that Laguna potters gathered at a local train depot in 1881 to sell small items. Bourke stated "the sugar bowls and salt cellars were bric-a-brac that would have set Eastern collectors crazy with envy[6]". Laguna potters were active in marketing pottery to tourists during the late 1800's and early 1900's. As the scene in Fig. 17 portrays, Laguna potters were still making large jars during this period.

Little Laguna pottery is available on the retail market. The older Laguna pieces are very collectable, rare, and demand a high price.

[6] Quote was contained in *New Mexico Magazine's* Special Edition, The Indian Arts of New Mexico, 1975, p.2.

215. Laguna Pueblo, ca 1915, E437.

Courtesy San Diego Museum of Man

216

217

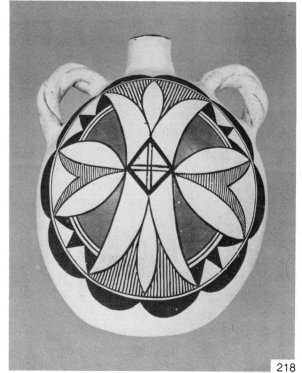

218

Fig. 216-218 Courtesy San Diego Museum of Man.; negatives 1000, 1977-33-1, 1974-45-1.

216. Laguna potter with ollas, ca 1882-1890.　　**217.** Laguna Pueblo jar. ca 1880-1900.　　**218.** Laguna Pueblo canteen. 1974.

220

221

222

223

Fig. 219-223 Courtesy San Diego Museum of Man; negatives 74461, 76324, 15418, 8943, 19908.

219. Laguna Pueblo. Evelyn Cheromiah. Indented design and white semi-matte. ca 1974.   **220.** Laguna Pueblo. Polychrome bowl. ca 1930.   **221.** Laguna Pueblo. Polychrome jar. ca 1930.   **222.** Laguna Pueblo. Historic Period.   **223.** Laguna Pueblo. Polychrome bowl, similar to design seen on same period Isleta pottery. ca 1920.

224

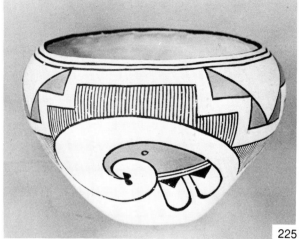

225

226

227

Fig. 224-227 Courtesy San Diego Museum of Man; negatives 10896, 73501, 8957, 281570.

224. Laguna Pueblo. Polychrome bowl. ca 1920. **225.** Laguna Pueblo. Evelyn Cheromiah. 1973. **226.** Laguna Pueblo. Fine polychrome olla. Historic Period. **227.** Laguna Pueblo. Polychrome pitcher. 1901-1922.

ZIA

Zia Pueblo has an uninterrupted history of producing fine pottery which is admired by both Indian and non-Indian. Their basalt and clay base pottery was a popular trade item with the Pueblos of Jemez, Santa Ana, and San Felipe. During the 1880's Zia depended upon pottery trade to obtain basic food items; to a lesser degree they still trade pottery with other Pueblos for necessities (White 1962). Zia Pueblo is wanting in productive agricultural lands and has relied upon trade for seasonal agricultural products. It is not uncommon to see Zia pottery displayed by another Pueblo potter.

Characteristically Zia polychrome pottery is distinctive but shares some similarities with Acoma pottery. Both Pueblos produce technologically fine ceramics. Zia pottery is thicker walled than Acoma's and the clay is gray with basalt rock temper. Acoma potters produce a greater assortment of types and styles. Zia decorations frequently include deer, bird and floral designs with red and black on a creamy white background. The base is solid red with a double banding encircling and separating the red base from the design area. Basalt, which is found in abundance at the Pueblo, is hand ground into fine grains by using a stone mano and metate. These grains are added to the clay as temper. Pots are thick-walled and serviceable. Black paint is obtained from a mineral and not the Rocky Mountain bee plant. This may be the same mineral used by some Jemez potters.

Active potters at Zia include Seferina Bell, Candelaria Gachupin, Helen Gachupin, Euseba Shije, Sofia Medina, Elizabeth Medina and Juanita Pino. Rafael and J.D. Medina are creating a distinctive, non-traditional style with acrylic painted designs. These designs of Pueblo dancers and eagles are expressed in fine detail using a multitude of colors. Their pottery has been featured in several major exhibits and seems to be accepted by the non-traditional collector.

228. Zia Pueblo, toward southeast from old site, ca 1915. Possibly Wesley Bradfield photo.

Fig. 229-231 Courtesy Pueblo One; 232 Courtesy Al Anthony; 233 Courtesy Nancy Daughters

229. Zia Pueblo. Polychrome olla. Early 20th Century. h 10¼". Private collection.   **230.** Zia Pueblo. Polychrome olla. Early 20th Century. h 10". Private collection.   **231.** Zia Pueblo. Polychrome olla. ca 1900. h 13½". The Collings Collection.   **232.** Zia Pueblo. Sofia Medina. Polychrome olla, pattern replicated three times. ca 1969. d 12", h 10½".   **233.** Zia Pueblo. Eusebia Shije. Polychrome. 1974. d 5½", h 4½". Nancy Daughters Collection.   **234.** Zia Pueblo. Helen Gachupin. Polychrome olla. 1979. d 8½", h 7¾".

Fig. 237 Courtesy Gila River Arts & Crafts Center

235. Zia Pueblo. Helen Gauchupin. Polychrome olla. 1979. d 10½'', h 9''.　　**236.** Zia Pueblo. J. Herera. Polychrome miniatures. 1979. h 1½''.

237. Zia Pueblo. Polychrome ollas. ca 1979. Sizes to d 11''.　　**238.** Zia Pueblo. Seferina Bell. Polychrome canteen. ca 1970. d 5½''.　　**239.** Zia Pueblo. Seferina Bell. Polychrome canteen. ca 1970. d 9''.　　**240.** Zia Pueblo. Juanito Pino. Polychrome olla. ca 1960. d 9½'', h 8⅜''.

Fig. 241 Courtesy Pueblo One; 242 Courtesy Bien Mur; 243 Courtesy Bill Ciesla; 245 Courtesy Marguerite Kernaghan; 246 Courtesy Audrey Greenough

241. Zia Pueblo. Juanito Pino. Polychrome olla. ca 1950. d 9½'', h 9½''.   **242.** Zia Pueblo. J. D. Medina. Acrylic painted ollas. (Left) ca 1979. d 11¾'', h 8''. (Center) ca 1979. d 11'', h 8''. (Right) d 10½'', h 8¼''.   **243.** Zia Pueblo. Rafael and Sofia Medina. Polychrome ollas. 1977. d 9'' to 10½''.   **244.** Zia Pueblo. Seferina Bell. Polychrome olla. ca 1965, d 10½'', h 9½''.   **245.** Zia Pueblo. (Left) Polychrome olla. Before 1960. d 10'', h 9''. (Center) Petra Lucero. Polychrome jar. (Right) Seferina Bell. Polychrome olla. ca 1960. d 10'', h 8''. (Center) Petra Lucero. Polychrome jar. (Right) Seferina Bell Polychrome olla. ca. 1960. d 10'', h 8''.   **246.** Zia Pueblo. Eusebia Shije. (Left) Polychrome jar. ca 1969. d 5'', h 4'' (Center) Eusebia Shije. Polychrome jar. ca 1969. d 1¾'', h 1½''. (Right) Eusebia Shije. Polychrome jar. ca 1969. d 4¼'', h 5''.

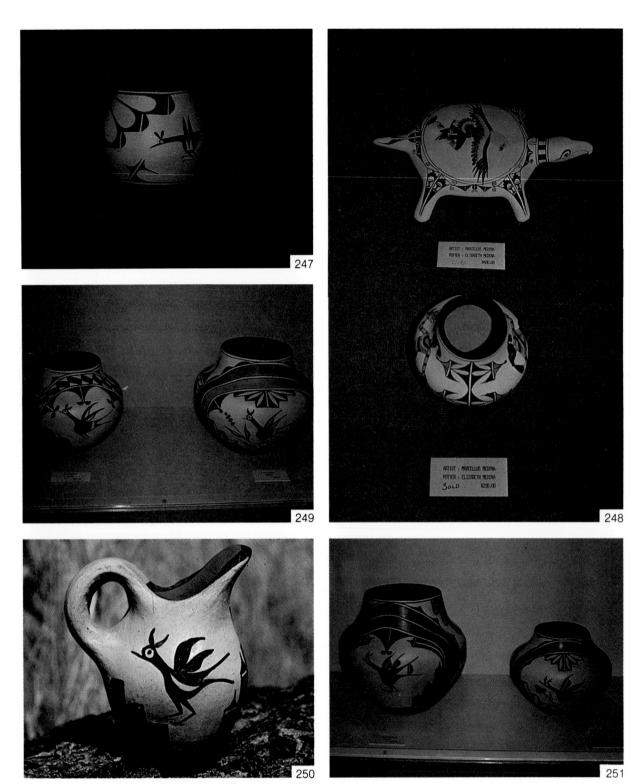

Fig. 248, 249, 251 Courtesy Pueblo Cultural Center; Fig. 250 Courtesy Bill Ciesla

247. Zia Pueblo. Eusebia Shije. Polychrome jar. ca 1974. d 5'', h 4¾''.   **248.** Zia Pueblo. Marcellus and Sofia Medina. 1979. **249.** Zia Pueblo. Sofia Medina. Polychrome jars. 1979.

250. Zia Pueblo. Sofia Medina. Miniature polychrome pitcher. ca 1977. d 2'', h 2¼''.   **251.** Zia Pueblo. Elizabeth Medina. Polychrome jars. 1979.

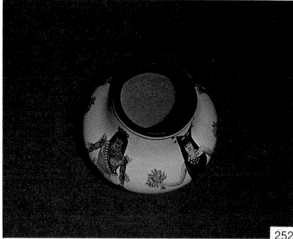

252

254

253

255

Fig. 253, 254 Courtesy Pueblo Cultural Center; 255 Courtesy Bien Mur

252. Zia Pueblo. Marcellus and Elizabeth Medina. Acrylic painted bowl. 1979.   **253.** Zia Pueblo. Elizabeth and Marcellus Medina. Acrylic painted bowl. 1979.   **254.** Zia Pueblo. Elizabeth and Marcellus Medina. Acrylic painted bowl. 1979.   **255.** Zia Pueblo. J. D. Medina. Acrylic painted bowl. 1979. d 10½'', h 8¼''.

SAN FELIPE

There is little evidence available that pottery was manufactured to any extent at San Felipe Pueblo. In all probability, the residents acquired most of their pottery from the nearby Pueblos of Zia, Cochiti, and Santo Domingo. There was little or no production of pottery during the 1960's. In 1979, a few potters were marketing a small red-on-tan tourist-type pot. There is nothing to suggest that ceramics will experience a revival at San Felipe in the near future.

SANTA ANA

Motivated by a sincere interest in the Santa Ana people, Mrs. Nancy Winslow of Albuquerque and Eudora Montoya of Santa Ana Pueblo spearheaded a pottery revival at Santa Ana. Their initial pottery class consisted of twenty potters—a relatively large group considering that the students reside in communities surrounding, but at the same distance from the ancient Pueblo. The result has been a slow revival of traditional Santa Ana pottery. A modest assortment of this pottery was on display at the 1979 Santa Fe Indian Market. It was impressive to see several potters represented such as Clara Paquin and Lena Garcia. Their enthusiasm and pride were apparent.

Traditional symbols on Santa Ana polychrome pottery represent turkey eyes, clouds, lightning, rainbows and headdresses. Santa Ana ware is similar to the red and black on cream polychrome pottery from its neighboring Zia Pueblo but the designs are bolder with less detail, and the tempering agent is fine sand while Zia's temper is basaltic rock.

Although the revival at Santa Ana has been slow, the pottery has been well received by the collector community and should continue to gain in quality and popularity.

256. San Felipe Pueblo, ca 1915-1920. Probably Wesley Bradfield photo.

256

257. Santa Ana Pueblo, South Side of Plaza, ca 1923.

257

Photos Courtesy San Diego Museum of Man, 2976 and 4231.

258

259

260

261

Fig. 259 Courtesy Pueblo Cultural Center; 260-261 Pueblo One.

258. Santa Ana Pueblo. Modern pottery on display at the 1979 Santa Fe Indian Market.   **259.** Santa Fe Pueblo. Eudora Montoya. Polychrome jar. 20th Century. h 12''.   **260.** Santa Ana Pueblo. Polychrome olla. ca 1910. d 11'', h 9½'   .   **261.** Santa Ana Pueblo. Polychrome olla, extensively restored. ca 1940. d 14'', h 13''.

SANTO DOMINGO

Santo Domingo Pueblo, with a population of over 2,000, is one of the largest Pueblos of the Southwest. It is known for its conservatism and the crafting of traditional turquoise and shell heishi necklaces. Santo Domingos value traditional ways and patterns, encourage use of their Keresan language, and actively practice organized communal ceremonies. They are active dancers and open their Pueblo to outsiders during their dance ceremonies. Their annual buffalo dance is a popular event attended by people from other Pueblos. The Santo Domingo Indian is an experienced trader at birth. In prehistoric times the Santo Domingo traders probably served as agents for other Rio Grande Pueblos in trading with the Plains and Coastal Indians. Some of their trading journeys may have lasted for six or more months at a time. By contrast, Santo Domingo traders today may accomplish their trading tasks in less than a week, traveling by jet across the United States.

Traditional necklaces are traded to the Navajo, other Pueblos, and to non-Indians. Evening dress attire in Southwest appropriately could include a Santo Domingo necklace.

This Pueblo was one of the prime participants in the Indian jewelry craze of the 1970's, producing silver jewelry of all descriptions. The rewards for this endeavor encouraged almost every able person at the Pueblo to produce silver jewelry and heishi necklaces. While other Pueblos were pursuing the concurrent pottery revival of the 1970's, Santo Domingo continued with jewelry.

Nevertheless, Santo Domingo has a high regard for pottery. It is common to see many old Santo Domingo pots displayed in homes along with pottery from other Pueblos. Traders who have pottery inventory provide a tempting barter.

Santo Domingo pottery is utilitarian but also frequently displayed at village festivities. It is a common practice to place initials on the bottom of pottery, in large painted letters, to identify the owner (Fig. 262). This should not be confused with the initials or signature of the maker. Most Santo Domingo pots made prior to 1960 did not bear identification marks of the maker. Their pottery which is easily distinguished from other Pueblo pottery is of two types, a black-on-red and a black-on-buff with a red base. A spirit break is included in the design on a traditional Santo Domingo ware. Bowls are the most common style. This year (1980) has seen a revival of a polished blackware by Cecelia M. Nieto. It is similar to the ca 1900 Santa Clara blackware.

There is relatively little pottery produced at Santo Domingo today. There are many women who know how to make pottery; however, for reasons unknown, they do not pursue the art. The Melchor family still produces a traditional black on red on a cream background. Santana Melchor, the most famous potter of this family produced pottery until her death in 1978. Another potter is reportedly making a black on polished red type pottery. Robert Tenorio is the only potter today making large traditional pots at the Pueblo. These have been very popular with collectors. He also makes smaller bowls, vases and canteens. During the first half of the 20th Century, Santo Domingo potters produced a variety of small pots, many with handles, for the tourist trade. Mostly these were scaled-down versions of their regular pottery, painted and decorated in traditional styles. Poster paints were used also during this period by some potters, but this type production seems to have ended. Large traditional jars and bowls were made prior to 1940. These are rare today and consequently collectable.

Santo Domingo has the capability of reviving its pottery tradition. As collector demand develops for the older Santo Domingo ceramic forms, more pottery may become available.

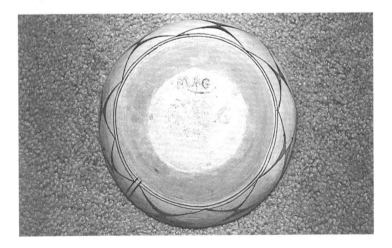

262. Markings (MXG) on the bottom of this Santo Domingo dough bowl are those of the owner, not the potter's mark.

Fig. 264 Courtesy Al Anthony; 265 Courtesy San Diego Museum of Man; 266 Courtesy Ike Lovato

263. Santa Domingo polychrome jar. ca 1930. d 10'', h 10''.   **264.** Santa Domingo Pueblo. Dough bowl. ca 1920. d 18'', h 9¾''.   **265.** Santo Domingo Pueblo. Scoop or ladle. ca 1930.   **266.** Santo Domingo Pueblo. Santana Melchor. A fine and rare shape pitcher. ca 1960. d 11'', h 4''.   **267.** Santo Domingo Pueblo. Polychrome bowl. ca 1930. d 11⅜'', h 5⅝''.

Fig. 268 Courtesy Pueblo Cultural Center; 269 Courtesy Pueblo One; 270 Courtesy Marguerite Kernaghan

268. Santo Domingo Pueblo. Polychrome bowl. ca. 1910. d 20'' h 12½''.　　**269.** Santo Domingo Pueblo. Polychrome bowl, ca 1900. d 16½'', h 8¼''.　　**270.** Santo Domingo Pueblo. Robert Tenorio. Polychrome bowl. ca 1978. d 8¼'', h 3¾''.　　**271.** Santo Domingo Pueblo. Robert Tenorio. Polychrome jar. 1979. d 9⅜'' h 9''. **272.** Santo Domingo Pueblo. Robert Tenorio. Canteen. 1979. d 5''.　　**273.** Santo Domingo Pueblo. Robert Tenorio. Pottery on display at the 1979 Santa Fe Indian Market.

Fig. 274 Courtesy Leon Hodge; 275 Bill Ciesla.

274. Santo Domingo Pueblo. Robert Tenorio. (Left) Bowl with handle. 1977. d 3½'', h 4''. (Right) Bowl with bird design. 1977. d 4½'', h 3¼''. **275.** Santo Domingo Pueblo. Tourist item. 1968. d 2¼'', h 3''. **276.** Domingo Pueblo. Polychrome bowl. ca 1950. d 6¾'', h 3¼''. **277.** Santo Domingo Pueblo. Polychrome bowl. ca 1940. d 8⅜'', h 4''. **278.** Santo Domingo Pueblo. Santana Melchor. Polychrome jar. ca 1977. d 3''.

279

280

281

282

283

Fig. 282, 283 Courtesy David Ichelson

279. Santo Domingo Pueblo. Santana Melchor. Polychrome jar. ca 1974. d 3¾'', h 4½''.   **280.** Santo Domingo Pueblo. Santana Melchor. Polychrome jar. ca 1977. d 4½'', h 4''.   **281.** Santo Domingo Pueblo. Marlene Melchor. Polychrome miniature. 1978. d 2½'', h 2''.   **282.** Santo Domingo Pueblo. (Right) Polychrome bowl with handle ca. 1930. d 5'', h 4''. (Left) Dolomita Melchor. pre 1950. d 3'', h 3''.   **283.** Santo Domingo Pueblo. Polychrome bowl. ca 1930. d 5'', h 4''.

COCHITI

Most Cochiti Pueblo pottery is pleasing although simplistically decorated. Designs usually include a "spirit break" similar to the "spirit break" included on Santo Domingo pots. Cochiti pottery is made following traditional methods. No Cochiti potter is known to depart from tradition in use of color and designs. In style, Cochiti potters have been creatively non-traditional.

Today Cochiti is known for ceramic storytellers developed by Helen Cordero. Painted with traditional paints of black and red on cream, these figurines consist of a mother covered by several children. Demand is great for Helen Cordero's figurines and those of other Cochiti potters such as Seferina Ortiz, Dorothy Trujillo, and Ada Suina.

Since 1900 Cochiti potters have found a ready market for animal figurines. One particularly characteristic figurine, commonly made by Cochiti potters, is the owl. In this respect there is a similarity of pottery figurines with Acoma, Jemez, and Zuni Pueblos.

Early Cochiti pottery was of two types, Kiva and Cochiti polychrome painted with red and black on cream. A form of the latter still is their traditional form of pottery today. Various designs are used including birds, animals, and symbols suggesting rain in the form of clouds and lightning.

Seferina Ortiz was instructed in the art of pottery making by her mother, Laurensita Herrera and has been producing pottery since 1968, using traditional designs on all her pottery. Appliques of lizards, frogs and turtles are frequently placed on her canteens and bowls. She also makes a navitity set which is simple but uniquely attractive and charming.

284. Cochiti Pueblo. ca 1905.

Courtesy San Diego Museum of Man, 2976.

285

286

287a.

287b.

288

289

Fig. 285-287B Courtesy Al Anthony; 288 Courtesy Fenn Galleries; 289 Courtesy Pueblo One

285. Cochiti Pueblo. Dorothy Trujillo. Polychrome storyteller. 1979. h 7''.　**286.** Cochiti Pueblo. Josephine Arquero. Storyteller figurines. 1979. h 8''.　**287(a)** and **287(b)** Cochiti Pueblo. Helen Cordero. Unusual and very collectable storyteller turtle. 1979. L 10½'', h 7''.　**288.** Cochiti Pueblo. Polychrome olla. ca 1900. h 10''.
289. Cochiti Pueblo. Rare bowl. Late 19th Century. d 15½'', h 7½''. Courtesy Pueblo One.

116

290. Cochiti Pueblo. Seferina Ortiz. 1979. h 3''.   **291.** Cochiti Pueblo. Seferina Ortiz. 1975. h 4''.
292. Cochiti Pueblo pottery on exhibit at 1979 Santa Fe Indian Market by Ortiz family.

Fig. 297, 298 Courtesy Indian Jewelry Center

293. Cochiti Pueblo. Seferina Ortiz. Nativity set. 1974. Figures up to 3½'' high.   **d 294.** Cochiti Pueblo. Seferina Ortiz. Storytellers. 1974. (Left) h 5''. (Right) h 6''.   **295.** Cochiti Pueblo. Seferina Ortiz. Canteen with appliqued figures. 1979. d 3¾''.   **296.** Cochiti Pueblo. Seferina Ortiz. Canteen with appliqued lizards. 1979. d 3¾''. **297.** Cochiti Pueblo. Signed Filipa. Storyteller. h 4''. Cochiti Pueblo.   **298.** Cochiti Pueblo. Ada Suina. Storyteller. h 6¼''.

JEMEZ

Jemez pottery, until recently, has been characteristically painted with poster paints and made for the casual tourist. Selling for less than $10.00 each, these pots had been made by several Jemez families since the 1930's. Roadside stands were common outlets with pottery being sold with Pueblo bread. With the increased interest in Pueblo arts and crafts over the past ten years, Jemez potters have been active in changing techniques and designs. There was not a single piece of Jemez poster paint pottery to be seen at the 1979 Santa Fe Indian Market's official booths. Neither have I seen poster paint pottery at Indian shops throughout the Southwest since 1979. However, some Jemez potters have begun to use acrylic paints to decorate pottery. These acrylic pots are attractive, painted in colors of orange, white and black with pleasing symmetrical designs on orange and buff backgrounds. Poster and acrylic paints are applied to pottery after firing.

Prior to the Great Pueblo Revolt of 1680 against the ruling Spaniards, Jemez produced a black-on-white pottery. Sherds of this style can be found scattered throughout the Jemez Pueblo landscape. Evelyn Vigil, a Jemez potter, is familiar with the technique of making the black-on-white pottery; however none currently is being produced. After the Revolt, Jemez relied upon pottery through trade with Zia. Close ties are maintained to the present day with Zia through trade and marriage. It is not uncommon to see Zia pots filled with cornmeal displayed in Jemez homes.

Most Jemez pottery is fired in electric kilns, although there are many potters who know how to fire outdoors. Jemez potters have been prominent in public shows over the past three years. It was reported that one potter received $1,500 for a bowl at the 1979 Indian Market. This represents a significant progression over a very short period from the $10.00 poster-painted tourist pots to highly collectable pieces.

Worth of special mention is the pottery produced by the Gachupin family. Their attractive pottery in natural tones has been received with enthusiasm by collectors. Marie Romero and her mother Persingula Gachupin have inspired the family to create a new style which is being adopted by others at Jemez. Their coiled bowls and vases, distinctive with geometric and corn designs are painted in orange and black on a textured light orange-buff background. Paints consist of a combination of clay, and gauco made from material collected near the Peublo. Clay and temper also are collected in the vicinity of Jemez and prepared in the traditional manner. Marie Romero and her daughters, Maxine Toya and Laura Gachupin, continue to experiment in designs and styles. Maxine and Laura are former students of the U.S. Department of the Interior's Institute of American Indian Arts of Santa Fe, New Mexico. At the Institute, their natural family-inspired abilities were developed through exposure to the expressive technique of creative contemporary arts. Returning to their Pueblo they have been an inspiration to their family and to others at the Pueblo, setting new trends.

Marie is known for her storytellers, wedding vases and sets of figures depicting Pueblo activities such as corn grinding and hunting. These sets, although uncomplicated in appearance, require considerable skill and patience to make.

Maxine specializes in fine detailed owls, clowns and kiva sets complete with human figures. She is a skillful painter as well as an outstanding potter.

Laura is known for her fine pots of various shapes with detailed geometric designs as well as an owl jar. The owl, in a squatted form, is made in a variety of sizes. Feathering is detailed by hand-molded pieces of clay. Another popular inspiration is a kiva bowl which may be polished or textured with designs on either or both surfaces. Her narrow-neck vases suggest an early Anasazi styling.

Three other Jemez potters, Evelyn Vigil, Juanita Toledo and Persingula M. Casiquito are making a style almost identical to the Pecos Glaze V pottery. This is discussed in the section on Pecos.

There are many young potters at Jemez who are experimenting with designs and techniques. With the success experienced by a few Jemez potters since 1977, more potters are being motivated and challenged toward excellence. New styles are expected to emerge from Jemez Pueblo as the overwhelming acceptance of the new Jemez pottery tradition continues to inspire others at the Pueblo.

Fig. 299 Courtesy Al Anthony, Adobe Gallery; 300-303 Courtesy Jemez State Monument and Museum of New Mexico; 304 Courtesy Audrey Greenough.

299. Jemez Pueblo. Juanita Fragua. "Kiva" bowl. 1978. d 6½", h 5¾".   **300.** Prehistoric. Jemez Black-on-White, Prayer meal bowl. ca. 1400 A.D.   **301.** Hitoric. Jemez Black-on-Gray, Seed bowl. ca 1600. **302.** Jemez Pueblo. Jemez Black-on-White, Bowl. ca. 1920.   **303.** Jemez Pueblo. Utility jar. ca 1923. **304.** Jemez Pueblo. Vangie Tofoya. (Left) Canteen. 1975. d 5". (Right) Wedding Vase. 1975 d 3½", h 6½". Audrey Greenough Collection.

Fig. 305 Courtesy Pueblo Cultural Center

305. Jemez Pueblo. E. Tsosie. Storyteller ca 1970. h 12''. **306.** Jemex Pueblo. Maxine Toya. Exceptional figurine ''Governor''.1979. h 6½''. **307.** Jemez Pueblo. Maxine Toya. Kiva with clowns. 1978. d 6½'', h 6''. **308.** Jemez Pueblo. Maxine Toya. Clown eating watermelon. 1979. h 2⅞''. **309.** Jemex Pueblo. Maxine Toya. Clown figurines. 1979. (Left) h 6''. (Center) h 2⅞''. (Right) h 6¼''. **310.** Jemez Pueblo. Maxine Toya. Owls. 1978. (Left h 3''. (Right) h 2''.

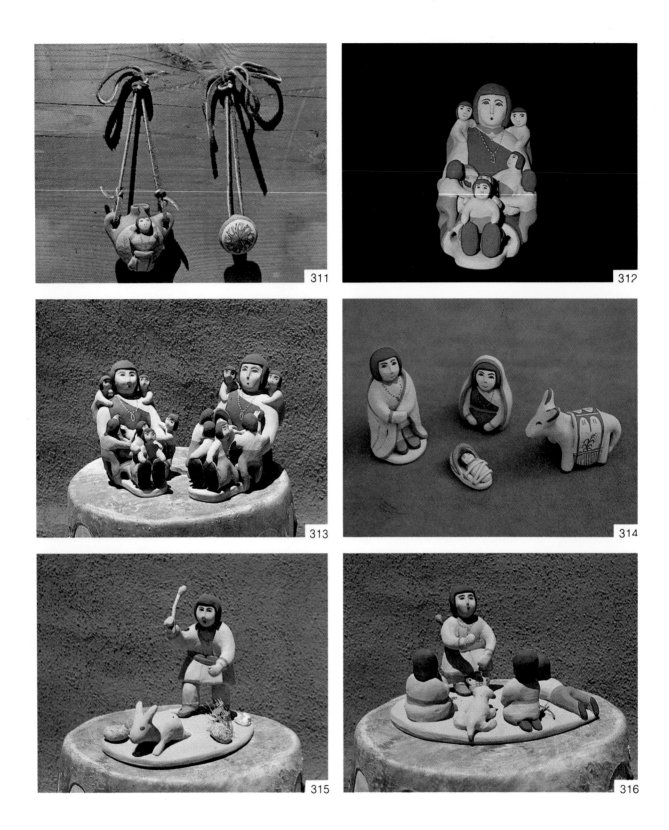

311. Jemez Pueblo. (Left) Marie Romero. Canteen. 1978. d 1½''. (Right) Maxine Toya. Pendant. 1979. d 1⅛''.
312. Jemez Pueblo. Marie Romero. Storyteller. 1978. 6''.   **313.** Jemez Pueblo. Marie Romero. Storyteller. 1979.
h 6-7''.   **314.** Jemez Pueblo. Marie Romero. Nativity Set. 1979. Largest figure h 3¼''.   **315.** Jemez Pueblo.
Marie Romero. ''Pueblo Hunter''. 1979. h 4''.   **316.** Jemez Pueblo. Marie Romero. ''Storytelling Time''. 1979 h 4''.

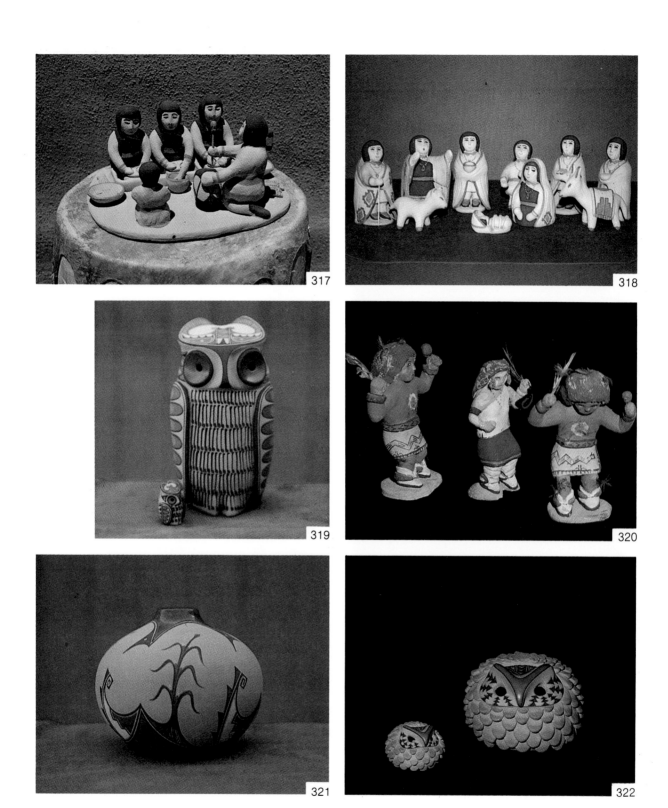

317. Jemez Pueblo. Marie Romero. "Corn Grinding Time." 1979. h 3½".   **318.** Jemez Pueblo. Marie Romero. Nativity set. 1979. h 4".   **319.** Jemez Pueblo. Maxine Toya. Owls. 1979. (Left) Miniature h 1½". (Right) h 8¾". **320.** Jemez Pueblo. Laura Gachupin. "Jemez Buffalo Dancers". 1977. h 4". This is the only set made and no price was given by the potter.   **321.** Jemez Pueblo. Laura Gauchupin. Large seed bowl. 1979. d 6¾", h 5⅝". **322.** Jemez Pueblo. Laura Gachupin. Owl jars, face of owl is a lid. 1978. (Left) d 3". (Right) d 7".

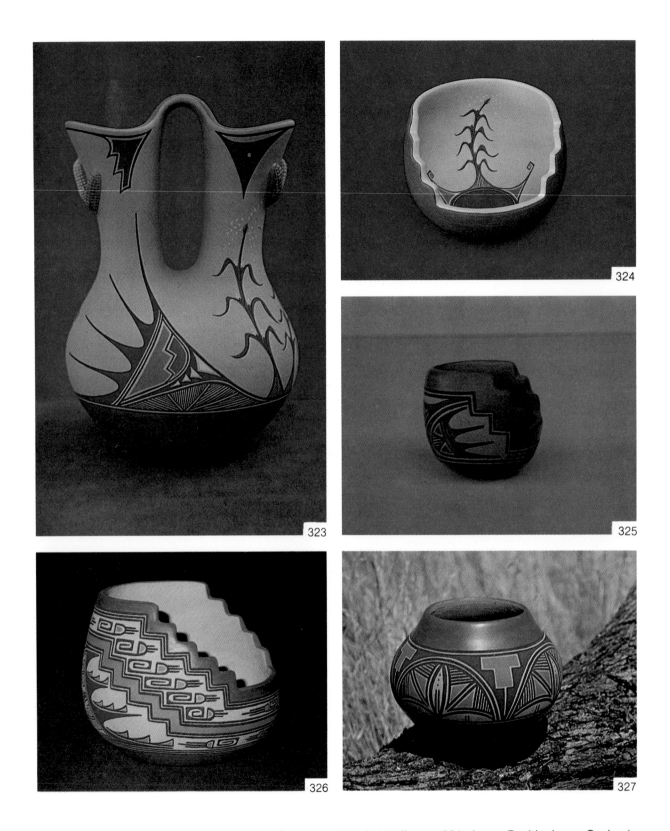

323. Jemez Pueblo. Laura Gachupin. Wedding vase. 1979. h 10½''. **324.** Jemez Pueblo. Laura Gachupin. Kiva bowl. 1979. d 6½'', h 4¾''. **325.** Jemez Pueblo. Laura Gachupin, Kiva bowl, miniature. 1978 d 2'', h 1¾''. **326.** Jemez Pueblo. Laura Gachupin. Kiva bowl. 1977. d 7½'', 6''. **327.** Jemez Pueblo. Laura Gachupin. Jar. 1977. d 6'', h 5½''

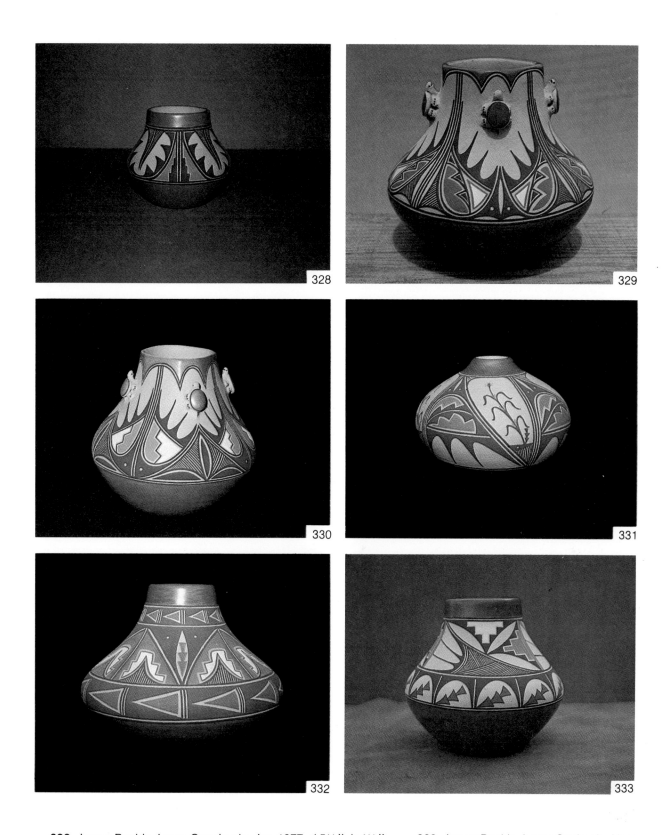

328. Jemez Pueblo. Laura Gauchupin. Jar. 1977. d 5½'', h 4½''.   **329.** Jemez Pueblo. Laura Gachupin. Vase with appliqued turtles. 1979. d 6½'', h 6''.   **330.** Jemez Pueblo. Laura Gachupin. Vase with appliqued turtles. 1978. d 6¾'', h 6''.   **331.** Jemez Pueblo. Laura Gachupin. Large seed bowl. 1979. d 6½'', h 5''.
332. Jemez Pueblo. Laura Gachupin. Vase. 1979. d 6½'', h 6''.   **333.** Jemez Pueblo. Laura Gachupin. Jar. 1979. d 6'', h 5¾''.

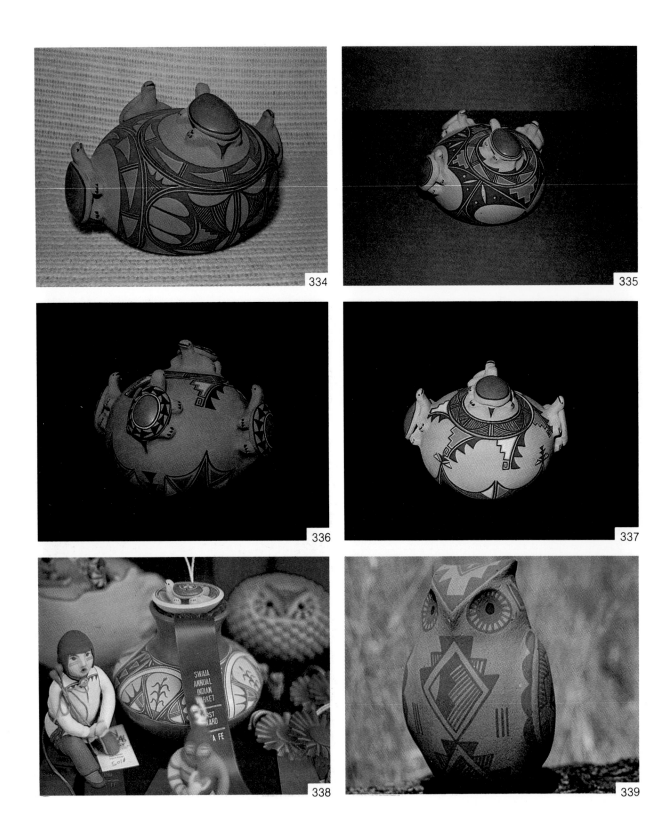

334. Jemez Pueblo. Laura Gachupin. Turtle bowl. 1979. d 8'', h 6''.　　**335.** Jemez Pueblo. Laura Gachupin. Turtle bowl. 1978. d 7½'', h 5''.　　**336.** Jemez Pueblo. Laura Gachupin. Turtle bowl. 1978. d 7½'', h 5''. **337.** Jemez Pueblo. Laura Gachupin. Turtle bowl. 1978. d 7⅜'', h 5¼''.　　**338.** Jemez Pueblo. Laura Gachupin. Turtle vase. 1979. d 7¼'', h 9¼''.　　**339.** Jemez Pueblo. Leona Fraqua. Owl. 1977. h 5''.

340

341

342

343

344

Fig. 342, 343 Courtesy Indian Jewelry Center

340. Jemez Pueblo. Miniature jars. 1979. h 1½'' to 2''.   **341.** Jemez Pueblo. Miniature bowl, acrylic paints. 1978.
342. Jemez Pueblo. Miniature bowls, acrylic paints. 1978. d½'' to 1½''.   **343.** Jemez Pueblo. Miniature bowls,
acrylic paints. 1978. d 1'' to 1⅝''.   **344.** Jemez Pueblo. Vase, acrylic paints, poor quality, h 17'', d 7¼''. ca 1970.

Fig. 346-349 Courtesy Indian Jewelry Center

345. Jemez Pueblo. V. Tafoya. Plate, acrylic paints. 1978. d 11''.   **346.** Jemez Pueblo. V. Tafoya. Bowl, acrylic paints. 1978. d 3'', h 1¾''.   **347.** Jemez Pueblo. V. Tafoya. Bowl. 1978. d 3'', h 1¾''. **348.** Jemez Pueblo. V. Tafoya. Vase, acrylic paints. 1979. d 2¼'', h 4''.   **349.** Jemez Pueblo. V. Tafoya. Vase, acrylic paints. 1979. d 4'', h 3''.   **350.** Jemez Pueblo. V. Tafoya. Wedding vase, acrylic paints. 1979. d 4'', h 6''.

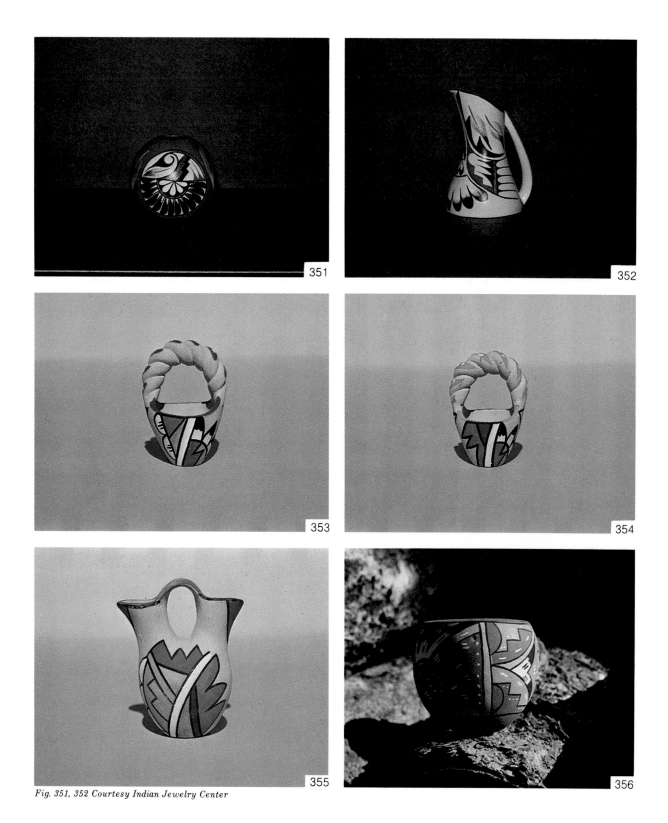

Fig. 351, 352 Courtesy Indian Jewelry Center

351. Jemez Pueblo. V. Tafoya. Bowl, acrylic paints. 1979. d 3½'', h 3½''.   **352.** Jemez Pueblo. V. Tafoya. Pitcher, acrylic paints. 1979. h 6''.   **353.** Jemez Pueblo. Poster painted bowl. ca 1979. h 2''. **354.** Jemez Pueblo. Poster painted bowl. ca 1979. h ''.   **355.** Jemez Pueblo. Poster painted wedding vase. 1973. h 4¾''.   **356.** Jemez Pueblo. Poster painted bowl. ca 1979. d 4'', h 4''.

Fig. 360, 361 Courtesy Bien Mur

357. Jemez Pueblo. Poster painted bowl. ca. 1979, d 3½'', h 6''.   **358.** Jemez Pueblo. Poster painted vase. ca 1970. d 5'', h 4''.   **359.** Jemez Pueblo. Poster painted wedding vase. ca 1960. h 3''.   **360.** Jemez Pueblo. Wedding vase, acrylic paints. 1979. d 9'', h 13½''.   **361.** Jemez Pueblo. Bess Yepa. 1979. (Left) d 6'', h 2¾''. (Center) Figurine h 3''. (Right) Figurine. d 2½'', h 5½''.

362. Jemez Pueblo. Persingula Gachupin. Jar. 1979. d 3'', h 2½''.   **363.** Jemez Pueblo. Persingula Gachupin. Jar. 1979. d 2¾'', h 2½''.   **364.** Jemez Pueblo. Persingula Gachupin. Bowl. 1979. d 2½'', h 1½''. **365.** Jemez Pueblo. Assortment of pots made by Bertha and Persingula Gachupin. 1978.   **366.** Jemez Pueblo. Bertha Gachupin. 1977. d 3'', h 3¼''.   **367.** Jemez Pueblo. (Left) Bertha Gachupin. Owl. 1979. h 2''. (Right) J. Fragua. 1979. h 1½''.   **368.** Jemez Pueblo. Bertha Gachupin. Jar. 1978. d 4'', h 3¾''.

PECOS

The ruins of Pecos Pueblo is a national monument administered by the U.S. Department of the Interior, National Park Service. Located approximately 18 miles southeast of Santa Fe, New Mexico, Pecos National Monument represents a fine example of the Federal Government's "living archaeology" concept discussed in Chapter III.

Although it is a small monument with an equally modest annual budget, monument personnel were able to initiate an experimental program with the objective of re-discovering the techniques of making the Pueblo Glaze V pottery. This was the pottery in use by Pecos Pueblo when the Spaniards arrived in the 16th Century. There were approximately 2000 inhabitants in 1583. When the Pecos were abandoned in 1838, there were only 17 persons. These took refuge with their distance relatives at Jemez. The Pecos pottery tradition and the Pecos culture were lost in this transition.

Interest in the Glaze V pottery by several persons resulted in a project with an aim to re-discover the techniques of making this pottery.

A volunteer worker, Lois Wittich Giles, conducted an exhaustive search for the materials used by Pecos potters to make and paint pottery. Meanwhile, National Park Service personnel located two potters at Jemez Pueblo with the skills to make coiled pottery following traditional methods. Jemez Pueblo seemed to be a logical location due to the ancestral association of Jemez and Pecos people. Evelyn Vigil and Juanita Toledo volunteered for the task. Evelyn, an accomplished potter, has an interest in the culture of her people and their pottery. She has provided inspiration to other Jemez potters. Assisted by Juanita, whose grandfather came from Pecos, Evelyn conducted an exhaustive search for clays, tempers, and paints. They experimented with techniques and firing methods. Louis Wittich Giles worked with these potters sharing their initial frustrations and disappointments. But their persistence resulted in final success of duplicating in detail the original Pecos Glaze V pottery. The techniques of preparing the clay, selecting and mixing the paints, polishing, decorating and particularily firing in an open firing pit with fir bark fuel were worked out. Pecos pottery is distinctive and easily distinguished from other pottery. It has a brown glaze paint which outlines the designs. The pottery base is red and the background of the design field is cream colored. A spirit break is included. This certainly is a modern day success story comparable to the achievements of Maria and Julian Martinez of San Ildefonso Pueblo with black-matte pottery and

that of Nampeyo and Hano in reviving ancient Sikyatki polychrome.[7]

Evelyn Vigil, Juanita Toledo, Rachael Loretto and Persingula M. Casiquito demonstrate the making of Pecos Glaze V pottery at Pecos National Monument during the summer months, June through August. Visitors can observe the entire process of making a Glaze V pot from preparation of the clay to firing. The potters are more than willing to answer questions and to explain details of the process. Pottery can be purchased directly from the potters at the momument.

370. Modern day potters. (Left) Persingula M. Casiquito and (Right) Evelyn Vigil recreating the Pecos Glaze V pottery as a demonstration project at Pecos National Monument following traditional methods. Note the beautifully shaped olla in the foreground on which Mrs. Vigil is ready to apply a design with a yucca brush. The steep angular base, although difficult to accomplish, is characteristic of this pottery.

369. Pecos National Monument, 1979.

[7] This information was provided by Evelyn Vigil and Persingula M. Casiquito on site at Pecos National Monument during August 1979. Ernest Ortega of Pecos National Monument also provided information. Supplemental information was obtained from Sheila Trysk's article (Trysk 1979).

371

373

372

Above Photos Courtesy Pecos National Monument and Museum of New Mexico.

371. Pecos Pueblo. Pecos Glaze V jar restored. 15th-16th century. d 12½ ″, h 9½ ″.   **372.** Pecos Pueblo. Pecos Glaze V Olla restored. 15th-16th century. d 16½ ″, h 10½ ″.   **373.** Pecos Pueblo. Pecos Glaze V bowl. 15th-16th century. d 9 ″, h 3¾ ″.

374. Pecos Pueblo. Modern creation of the Pecos Glaze olla by Jemez potter Persingula M. Casiquito. 1979. d 10'', h 7½''.   **375.** Pecos Pueblo. Evelyn Vigil pot. This one made in 1979 cracked during firing. d 11'', h 9''.
376. Pecos Pueblo. Modern bowl with swastika design. 1979. d 5''.   **377.** Pecos Pueblo. Modern day pots for sale by potters at Pecos National Monument, 1979.   **378.** Pecos Pueblo. Modern pots. (Left) Evelyn Vigil. Bowl with El Capitan design. 1979. d 4¾'', h1¾''.   **379.** Pecos Pueblo. Modern day pots for sale by potters at Pecos National Monument. 1979.

TESUQUE

Tesuque Pueblo has produced high-quality pottery at least since the early 19th Century. Powhoge, Tesuque, and Tatunque Polychromes are examples of their pottery tradition. A black-on-red also was made around the turn of the Century.

Perhaps, the most famous ceramics from Tesuque are the "rain gods". This form has no religious significance. The Gunther Candy Company of Chicago marketed these tourist "rain gods" ceramics beginning in the late 1890's. Since the 1930's, Tesuque "rain gods" have been decorated with bright color poster paints and acrylics while previously they were decorated with traditional paints. Manuel Vigil who is in his nineties still makes nativity figure sets decorated in Plains Indian or Pueblo style dress, painted with bright poster paints. These have become popular with collectors, as they represent a form of New Mexico folk art (Monthan 1979). Priscilla Vigil has made the more traditional Tesuque bowls and jars but it is doubtful that she has made any in recent years. Lorencita Pino has produced a few of the old Tesuque style pots during the past decade. Anna Maria Lovato is creating pottery with red on textured-tan surface which differs from any previous Tesuque style. Sorenata Pino is another potter who has been active in the past decade.

All traditional style Tesuque pots are rare and in demand by collectors and museums.

380. Tesuque Pueblo potter making the tourist "rain god" figurine.

381. Tesuque Pueblo. Fine example of Tatunque Polychrome olla. ca 1890. d 12½", h 10½".

135

382

383

384

385

Fig. 382 Courtesy San Diego Museum of Man; 383 Courtesy Marguerite Kernaghan

382. Tesuque Pueblo jar. Historic Period.   **383.** Tesuque Pueblo. Tourist "Rain god" figurines (Left) Marie Herrera. Made in 1920's and kept by Marie Herrera until 1979 when it was repainted and sold to the Marguerite Kernaghan Collection. h 6½". (Right) ca 1930. h 7".   **384.** Tesuque Pueblo. Tourist "Rain god" figurine. ca 1970. h 6".   **385.** Tesuque Pueblo. Manuel Vigil. Nativity set, poster painted figurines. This is a very collectable New Mexico folk art item. 1974.

386

388

Fig. 388 Courtesy San Diego Museum of Man

387

386. Tesuque Pueblo. Tourist bowl. Practice of painting design in blue or purple was common in 1930's.
387. Tesuque Pueblo. Anna Marie Lovato. Miniature bowls, recent style. 1979. (Left) d 2½'', h 1¾''. (Center) d 3½'',
h 1½'' (Right) d 2¼'', h 1''.　　**388.** Tesuque Pueblo. Polychrome vase. ca 1970.

NAMBE AND POJOAQUE

Today the Pueblos of Nambe and Pojoaque share a common interest in contemporary ceramics. Their original pottery tradition ceased long before its present revival. Polished pots both red and black, had been made at Nambe and probably at Pojoaque. Nambe also made micaceous clay pottery similar to that of Taos and Picuris until the late 1940's (Harlow 1977).

The pottery revival at Nambe and Pojoaque over the past decade has produced a high-quality ware similar in many respects to pottery from Santa Clara Pueblo. Polychrome pottery finished either in a textured matte or a polished background currently is popular. Nambe and Pojoaque potters also make a polished redware and a polished blackware. Potters who have demonstrated a high level of technical excellence and imagination include Joseph and Thelma Talachy and Virginia Gutierrez. Joseph and Thelma occasionally make a jar fashioned after the 18th Century Pojoaque polychrome. Two excellent examples can be seen at the Museum of New Mexico.[8]

---

[8] Personal communications with Joseph and Thelma Talachy.

389. Nambe/Pojoaque Pueblo. Virginia Gutierrez. Polychrome plate. 1979. d 11¾''. 390. Nambe/Pojoaque Pueblo. Virginia Gutierrez. Polychrome vase. 1979. d 7½'', h 6''. 391. Nambe/Pojoaque Pueblo. Virginia Gutierrez. Polychrome seed bowl. 1979. d 7'', h 2⅜''. 392. Nambe/Pojoaque Pueblo. Virginia Gutierrez. Polychrome vase. 1980. d 6½'', h 7½''.

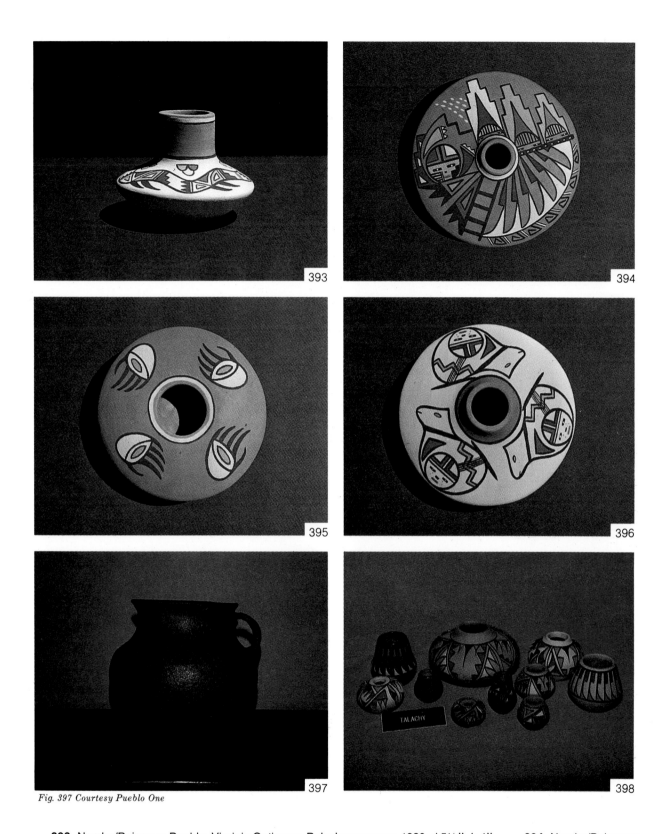

393

394

395

396

397

398

Fig. 397 Courtesy Pueblo One

393. Nambe/Pojoaque Pueblo. Virginia Gutierrez. Polychrome vase. 1980. d 5½'', h 4''.   **394.** Nambe/Pojoaque Pueblo Virginia Gutierrez. Polychrome seed bowl. 1980. d 7⅜'', h 2¾''.   **395.** Nambe/Pojoaque Pueblo. Virginia Gutierrez Polychrome seed bowl. 1980. d 5⅝'', h 1¾''.   **396.** Nambe/Pojoaque Pueblo. Virginia Gutierrez. Polychrome seed bowl. 1980. d 7¾'', h 8¾″.   **397.** Nambe Pueblo. Josefita Anaya. ca 1935. d 9¾'', h 3¾''. **398.** Pojoaque Pueblo. Joe and Thelma Talachy. Assortment of styles. 1973-1979.

Fig. 403, 404 Courtesy Indian Jewelry Center

399. Pojoaque Pueblo. Joe and Thelma Talachy. Miniature olla. 1977. d 2¾'', h 2¼''.   **400.** Pojoaque Pueblo. Joe and Thelma Talachy. Polychrome olla. 1979. d 7¾'', h 6¼''.   **401.** Pojoaque Pueblo. Joe and Thelma Talachy. Polychrome seed bowl. 1978. d 3'', h 2''.   **402.** Pojoaque Pueblo. Joe and Thelma Talachy. Polychrome vase, textured. 1979. d 2'', h 1½''.   **403.** Pojoaque Pueblo. Joe and Thelma Talachy. Miniature polychrome olla with feather design. 1977. d 2¼'', h 2⅜''.   **404.** Pojoaque Pueblo. Joe and Thelma Talachy. Miniature polychrome vase, feather design. 1978. d 2½'', h 2¼''.

Fig. 405-407 Courtesy Indian Jewelry Center Fig. 409 Courtesy Bill Klein

405. Pojoaque Pueblo. Joe and Thelma Talachy. Miniature Polychrome olla. 1979. d 2'', h 1½''.   **406.** Pojoaque Pueblo. Joe and Thelma Talachy. Miniature polychrome jar. 1979. d 1½'', h 1¼''.   **407.** Pojoaque Pueblo. Joe and Thelma Talachy. Miniature vase. 1977. d1⅜'', h 2¾''.   **408.** Pojoaque PUeblo. Joe and Thelma Talachy. Polychrome bowl. 1973.   **409.** Pojoaque Pueblo. Joe and Thelma Talachy. Turtle. 1979. L 3¼''.   **410.** Pojoaque Pueblo. Joe and Thelma Talachy. Polychrome bowl. 1973. d 5⅜'', h 3⅝''.

SANTA CLARA

Santa Clara Pueblo has more potters and produces more pottery than any other Pueblo. Names such as Teresita Naranjo, Margaret Tafoya, Margaret and Luther Gutierrez, Belen Tapia, Minnie Vigil, and Joseph Lonewolf are well known to students of Indian art. Their blackware shares equal popularity with that of San Ildefonso Pueblo. Santa Clara potters produce various styles, types, colors and sizes ranging from the large traditional ollas to polychrome and fine incised miniatures. The black-matte or black-on-black style perfected by Maria and Julian at San Ildefonso was not made at Santa Clara until 1927. A black utility ware not to be confused with the Maria and Julian style, however, was produced at Santa Clara and other Pueblos during the historic period. Polished redware also is a popular style at Santa Clara.

After 1880, Santa Clara increased the number of styles. This coincides with the arrival of a rail line between Espanola and Santa Fe which resulted in increased tourism and commerce.

Easy access to Santa Clara Pueblo located at the edge of Espanola, New Mexico, results in heavy tourist trade in the summer. Additionally traders frequent the Pueblo weekly where they usually find an excellent selection of fine pottery. Pottery buyers, whether tourist or trader, are welcomed by these friendly people. Betty LeFree lists 89 potters at Santa Clara in 1975 (LeFree 1975). Today the number may exceed 200.

Imagination of the Santa Clara potters shows no limits; however, each person retains a degree of traditionalism in style which can be identified readily with the specific potter. Individuals familiar with Santa Clara pottery usually can name the potter without scrutinizing the name inscribed on the bottom of the pot. Almost all Santa Clara pottery made today is signed. These potters take great pride in their work. If there were such a thing a competition at the Pueblos, it exists in a friendly manner at Santa Clara. Examples of unique styles can be illustrated best by listing a few of the potters.

Petra Gutierrez, an accomplished potter, is the mother of Minnie Vigil, Thelma Talachy, Gloria Garcia, and Lois Guiterrez. This well known pottery family has set new trends at the Pueblos.

411. Santa Clara Pueblo. ca 1915. Possibly Wesley Bradfield photo.

Courtesy San Diego Museum of Man

142

Minnie Vigil is a prolific potter always willing to share her enthusiasm with visitors. Her variety of styles is equaled only by her level of production. Minnie is best known for her polychromes which might be fashioned with a textured surface or a highly-polished finish in black, olive, white, buff and red. Most of her pots show representative designs with a preference for jar and seed bowl shapes. She experiments constantly with new styles and colors.

Gloria Garcia (Goldenrod) also makes incised pottery in black and red. Designs of deer, bison, antelop, eagle, butterflies and elk are accented with stones of coral or turquoise. Many are shaped as miniature seed bowls or minature water jugs. Goldenrod's husband, John, an artist in oil and canvas media, sometimes assists in the designs of Goldenrod's pottery.

Virginia Ebelacker specializes in black polished ollas but also makes boxes, bowls and plates. Large pots require patience and technical skills and only a few can be made each year. Virginia learned from her mother Margaret Tafoya and both incorporate traditional Santa Clara bearpaw and rainbow designs in their pots.

Teresita Naranjo, Celestina Naranjo, and Stella Chavarria make both red and black carved pots finished in a high polish and carved with precision and detail.

Helen Shupa also is known for her carved blackware. Belen Tapia is known for her redware and polychrome pots with effective use of a gray-blue paint. Belen's daughter, Anita Suazo, shares an outstanding reputation.

Many Santa Clara potters are related either to the Tafoya or the referenced Gutierrez families. The Camilio Tafoya family, represented by Camilio, Sunflower, Joseph Lonewolf, Rosemary Lonewolf and Grace Medicine Flower creates incised pottery in red, black and black burnish. Detailed designs are incised on the pots, and frequently are integrated into the designs. This combination is especially sought after by collectors. The Youngbloods of the Tafoya family are known for their versatility in shapes and highly polished blackware.

Santa Clara Pueblo potters should take great pride in their contributions to sustaining the ceramic arts of the Pueblos. Their high levels of technical excellence and unbounded imagination have added to bringing focus on Pueblo ceramics.

Courtesy Smithsonian Institution, 4566.

412. Santa Clara Pueblo, Nestoria Naranjo with black olla, 1916.

413

414

415

416

417

Fig. 414, 415 Courtesy Al Anthony

413. Santa Clara Pueblo. Celestina Naranjo. Black beaver. 1974. h 3¾''. U.S. Army Photograph.
414. Santa Clara Pueblo. Margaret and Luther Gutierrez. Nativity set (Nacimiento). 1979. Tallest figure 4½''.
415. Santa Clara Pueblo. Art and Martha Cody (Haungooah). Incised bowl. 1975. d 2½'', h 2''.
416. Santa Clara Pueblo. (Left) Mary Cain. ca 1960. d 3½'', h 2⅝''. (Right) Belen Tapia. ca 1960. d 4'', h 2⅝''. Audrey Greenough Collection. **417.** Santa Clara Pueblo. Anita Suazo. Fine polished black lidded jar with bear paw imprint. d 8'', h 7''.

418

419

420

418. Santa Clara Pueblo. Celestina Naranjo. Black carved turtle. 1974. Length 3½''. U.S. Army Photograph.
419. Santa Clara Pueblo. Virginia Ebelacker. Fine wedding vase with traditional bear paw design. 1974. d 3½'', h 6½''. U.S. Army Photograph.   **420.** Santa Clara Pueblo pottery showing a variety of blackware styes, 1974. U.S. Army Photograph.

145

421

422a.

422b.

423

424

425

Fig. 423, Courtesy Audrey Greenough

421. Santa Clara Pueblo. Stella Chavarria. Blackware carved feather design. 1974. d 5'', h 4¾''. U.S. Army Photograph.   **422a** and **422b.** Santa Clara Pueblo. Minnie Vigil. Polychrome seed bowl. ca 1977. d 5'', h 3½''. **423.** Santa Clara Pueblo. Black and Black-matte miniatures. 1940-1960. Audrey Greenough Collection. **424.** Santa Clara Pueblo. Dorothy Gutierrez. Nativity set. Figure to 3'' high. ca 1976.   **425.** Santa Clara Pueblo. Goldenrod. Incised seed bowl, water serpent design. 1979. d 2¼'', h 1¼''.

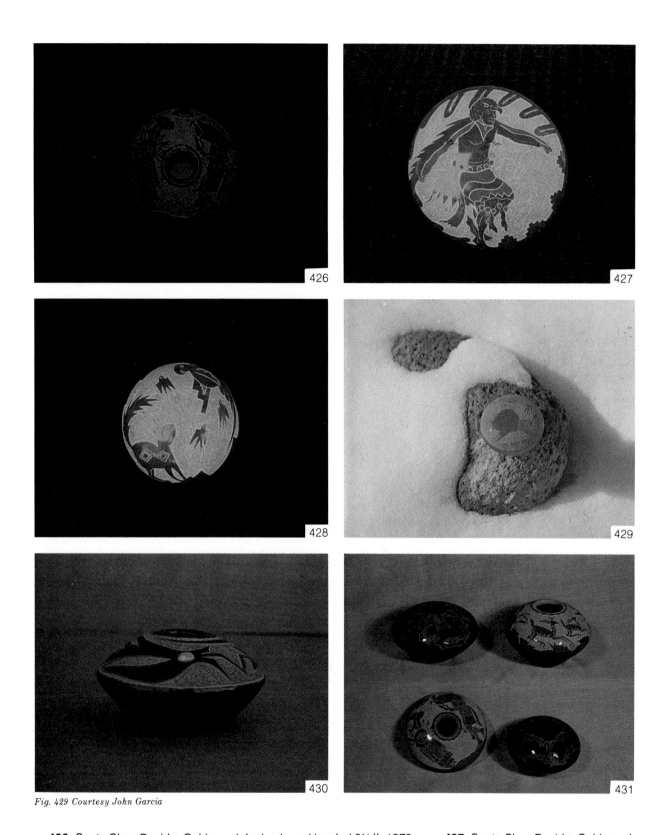

Fig. 429 Courtesy John Garcia

426. Santa Clara Pueblo. Goldenrod. Incised seed bowl. d 3½''. 1979.   **427.** Santa Clara Pueblo. Goldenrod. Eagle dancer. 1980 d 2⅝'', h 1½''.   **428.** Santa Clara Pueblo. Goldenrod. Incised wolf and parrot design. 1979. **429.** Santa Clara Pueblo. Goldenrod. Buffalo design. 1978 d 2'', h 1''.   **430.** Santa Clara Pueblo. Goldenrod. 1978. d 2⅞'', h 1½''.   **431.** Santa Clara Pueblo. Goldenrod. 1978. d 3½'' to 3⅝''.

Fig. 435, 437 Courtesy Indian Jewelry Center; 436 Courtesy Indian Village

432. Santa Clara Pueblo. Goldenrod. 1980. Vase with bear paw design. d 1½'', h 1¾''.   **433.** Santa Clara Pueblo. Goldenrod. Corn Maiden. 1980. d 2'', h 2½''.   **434.** Santa Clara Pueblo. Goldenrod. Corn maiden. 1980. d 2⅝'', h 2''.   **435.** Santa Clara Pueblo. Goldenrod. 1979. d 1¾'', h 1¼''.   **436.** Santa Clara Pueblo. Goldenrod. Horny toad design on vase. 1980. d 2½'', h 2⅜''.   **437.** Santa Clara Pueblo. Goldenrod. 1979. d 2'', h 2½''.

438

439

440

441

442

443

Fig. 443 Courtesy John Garcia

438. Santa Clara Pueblo. Goldenrod. 1980. d 3¼'', h 2¼''.   **439.** Santa Clara Pueblo. Goldenrod. Buffalo designs. 1980. d 2¾'', h 1⅜''.   **440.** Santa Clara Pueblo. Goldenrod. Eagle design. 1980. d 2⅜'', h 1⅝''.   **441.** Santa Clara Pueblo. Goldenrod. Flute player design. 1980. d 2¾'', h 1½''.   **442.** Santa Clara Pueblo. Goldenrod. Buffalo dance design. 1980. d 3½'', h 1¾''.   **443.** Santa Clara Pueblo. Goldenrod. Bowls with incised butterfly designs. 1975.

Fig. 444-448 Courtesy John Garcia; 449 Courtesy Dave Ichelson

444. Santa Clara Pueblo. Goldenrod. 1977. d 2'' to 3''.   **445.** Santa Clara Pueblo. Goldenrod. 1977. d 1¾'', h 2''.   **446.** Santa Clara Pueblo. Goldenrod. 1977. d 1¾'', H 2¼''.   **447.** Santa Clara Pueblo. Goldenrod. 1980. d 5⅝'' to 2¼''.   **448.** Santa Clara Pueblo. Goldenrod. 1980. d 1¾'' to 2¼''.   **449.** Santa Clara Pueblo. Carved black-ware. ca. 1975. d 5¼'', h 4¼''.

Fig. 452 Courtesy Nancy Daughters

450. Santa Clara Pueblo. Juanita. "Wo-Peen". Bowl, redware. ca 1930. d 6", h 4". **451.** Santa Clara Pueblo. Fidel. "Onquan Peen" Archuleta. 1973. d 4¼", h 3". **452.** Santa Clara Pueblo. Elizabeth Naranjo. Black-ware bowl, squash or melon design. 1974. d 6", h 4¾". **453.** Santa Clara Pueblo. Joann Million. Black-ware with indented rim. 1973. d 3¾", h 3⅝" **454.** Santa Clara Pueblo. Redware jar with lid. 1974. d 1¾", h 2½". **455.** Santa Clara Pueblo. Geneva Suazo. Black-matte bowl. 1975. d 5", h 3⅛".

456. Santa Clara Pueblo. Margaret Geneva. Black-matte bowl. 1975. d 5'', h 3½''. 457. Santa Clara Pueblo. Margaret Tafoya. Carved bowl. ca 1950. d 6'', h 9''. 458. Santa Clara Pueblo. Richard Ebelacker. Carved black-ware bowl. 1974. d 7'', h 4''. 459. Santa Clara Pueblo. Virginia Ebelacker. Turtle. 1974. L 5¼''. 460. Santa Clara Pueblo. Virginia Ebelacker. Water jar with bear paw imprint. 1979. d 5¼'', h 4½''. 461. Santa Clara Pueblo. Virginia Ebelacker. Carved plate with bear paws. 1974. d 11¾''.

462

463

464

465

466

467

Fig. 463 Courtesy Nancy Daughters

462. Santa Clara Pueblo. Virginia Ebelacker. Water jar with bear paw imprint. 1974. d 7½'', h 7¾''.   **463.** Santa Clara Pueblo. Margaret and Luther Gutierrez. 1975. d 2½'', h 2¾''.   **464.** Santa Clara Pueblo. Margaret and Luther Gutierrez. 1974. Turtle. d 5½''. Racoon. h 3''.   **465.** Santa Clara Pueblo. Anita Suazo. Carved black-ware bowl. 1979. d 3⅜'', h 2⅛''.   **466.** Santa Clara Pueblo. Anita Suazo. Fine carved turtle. 1979. L 6'', h 4''. **467.** Santa Clara Pueblo. Anita Suazo. Carved red-ware. 1979. d 4'', h 2½''.

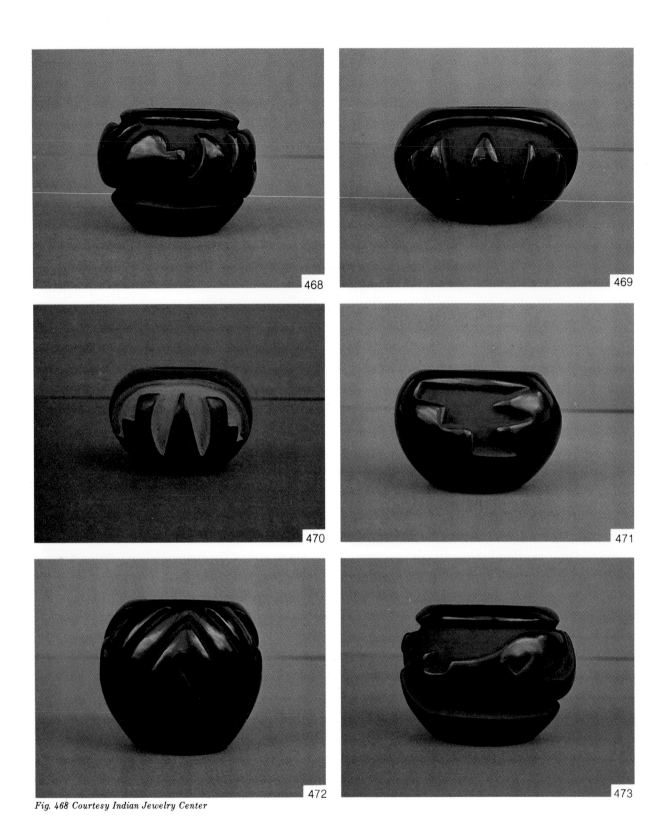

468

469

470

471

472

473

Fig. 468 Courtesy Indian Jewelry Center

468. Santa Clara Pueblo. Anita Suqzo. Carved bowl. 1979. d 3½'', h 2¼''.　　**469.** Santa Clara Pueblo. Anita Suazo. Carved bowl. d 3¾'', h 2⅛''.　　**470.** Santa Clara Pueblo. Anita Suazo. Carved red-ware bowl. 1979. d 3'', h 2''.　　**471.** Santa Clara Pueblo. Anita Suazo. Triangular carved bowl. 1979. d 3'', h 2½''.　　**472.** Santa Clara Pueblo. Anita Suazo. Carved black-ware jar. 1979. d 3'', h 2½''.　　**473.** Santa Clara Pueblo. Anita Suazo. Carved bowl. 1979. d 3⅜'', h 2⅜''.

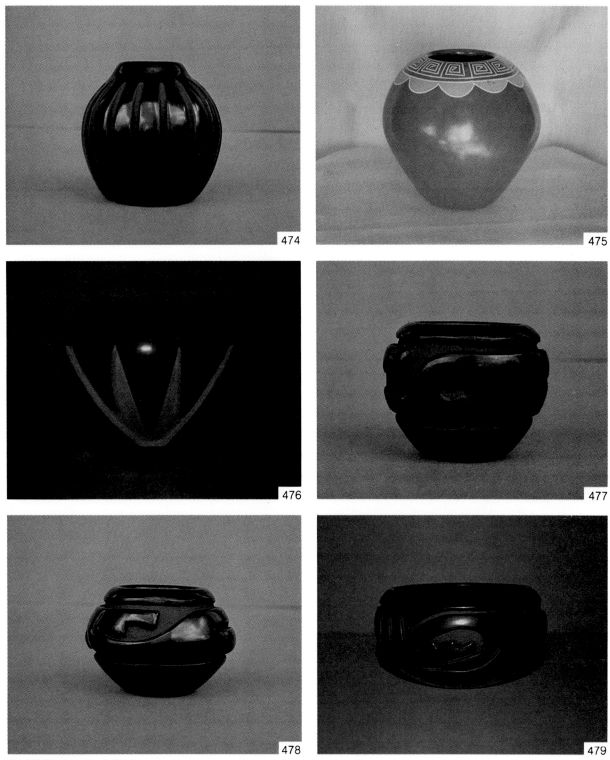

Fig. 475 Courtesy David Ichelson

474. Santa Clara Pueblo. Anita Suazo. Black-ware jar with melon design. 1979. d 3'', h 3''.　　**475.** Santa Clara Pueblo. Belen Tapia. Polychrome seed bowl. 1974. d 5½'', h 5''.　　**476.** Santa Clara Pueblo. Belen Tapia. Carved bowl. 1973. d 6¼'', h 5''.　　**477.** Santa Clara Pueblo. Stella Chavarria. Carved bowl. 1977, d 2¾'', h 2⅛''. **478.**Santa Clara Pueblo. Stella Cavarria. Carved bowl. 1975. d 2¾'', h 1¾''.　　**479.** Santa Clara Pueblo. Stella Chavarria. Carved bowl. 1974. d 7'', h 3½''.

480

481

482

483

484

485

Fig. 482 Courtesy Jerry & Dorothy Guinand; 483 Courtesy Bob LaPerriere; 485 Courtesy Nancy Daughters

480. Santa Clara Pueblo. Stella Chavarria. Carved bowl. 1975. d 6″, h 3-5/8″.   **481.** Santa Clara Pueblo. Stella Chavarria. Black carved feather design vase. 1977. h 4''.   **482.** Santa Clara Pueblo. Mida Tafoya. 1965. d 7⅝'', h 4¼''.   **483.** Santa Clara Pueblo. Art Coty. Incised redware. 1978. d 1½'', h 1''. **484.** Santa Clara Pueblo. Faustina Gutierrez. Black-matte vase. ca 1950.   **485.** Santa Clara Pueblo. Lois Gutierrez. Polychrome jar. 1979. d 7'', h 7''.

156

Fig. 486, 491 Courtesy Nancy Daughters; 488, 490 Courtesy Indian Jewelry Center

486. Santa Clara Pueblo. Lois Gutierrez. Polychrome jar. 1979. d 7'', h 7''.   **487.** Santa Clara Pueblo. Lois Gutierrez. Polychrome jar. 1977. d 7½'', h 6''.   **488.** Santa Clara Pueblo. Santanita Suazo. 1975. d 2⅞'', h 2¼''. **489.** Santa Clara Pueblo. Santanita Suazo. Rectangular bowl. 1977. d 2⅝'', h 2''.   **490.** Santa Clara Pueblo. Santanita Suazo. 1978. L 2¾''.   **491.** Santa Clara Pueblo. Mary Gutierrez. Incised hummingbird design. 1979. d 2½'', h 2⅝''.

Fig. 496, 497 Courtesy Marguerite Kernaghan

492. Santa Clara Pueblo. Eloy Naranjo. Bear figurine, turquoise stones for eyes, also note the "heart line". 1978. L 4½". **493.** Santa Clara Pueblo. Celestina Naranjo. Black bowl with bear paw imprint. 1974. d 5", h 3¼". **494.** Santa Clara Pueblo. Celestina Naranjo. Polychrome jar. 1977. d 2⅜", h 2⅛". **495.** Santa Clara Pueblo. Celestina Naranjo. Black-matte. 1977. (Left) d 3½", h 1½". (Right) d 4", h 4¼". **496.** Santa Clara Pueblo. Christina Naranjo. Avanyu or feathered serpent design on black jar. 1978. d 7", h 5½". **497.** Santa Clara Pueblo. Flora Naranjo. Black-matte jar. 1977. d 4", h 2½".

498

499

500

501

502

503

Fig. 498, 499 Courtesy Bien Mur

498. Santa Clara Pueblo. (Left) Elizabeth Naranjo. Black carved jar. 1979. d 8'', h 8''. (Right) Mary Singer. Black carved vase. d 10'', h 12½''.　　**499.** Santa Clara Pueblo. Sally Gutierrez. 1979. (Left vase) d 4'', h 3¼''. (Left wedding vase) h 8¼''. (Small wedding vase) h 4¼''. (Right bowl) d 5'', h 2¾''.　　**500.** Santa Clara Pueblo. Dorothy Gutierrez. 1979. L 3''.　　**501.** Santa Clara Pueblo. Dorothy Gutierrez. 1977. Nativity set. h 3''.　　**502.** Santa Clara Pueblo. Dorothy Gutierrez. Black-matte mud heads. 1979. (Left to Right) h 1¼'', h 2¼'', h 1''.　　**503.** Santa Clara Pueblo. Dorothy Gutierrez. Beaver figurines. 1979. L 4''.

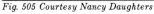

Fig. 505 Courtesy Nancy Daughters

504. Santa Clara Pueblo. Dorothy Gutierrez. Beaver figurines. 1979. h 2''.   **505.** Santa Clara Pueblo. Minnie Vigil. Jar with bear paw design. 1974. d 7'', h 4¾''.   **506.** Santa Clara Pueblo. Minnie Vigil. Polychrome wedding vase. 1977. h 8''.   **507.** Santa Clara Pueblo. Minnie Vigil. Styles and shapes. 1977 to 1979.   **508.** Santa Clara Pueblo. Minnie Vigil. 1978. (Left) Jar. d 4''. (Center) Seed bowl. d 4''. (Right) Bowl. d 7''.   **509.** Santa Clara Pueblo. Minnie Vigil. Seed bowl. 1978. d 3¼'', h 2½''.

510 511 512 513 514 515

510. Santa Clara Pueblo. Minnie Vigil. Seed bowl. 1979. d 3″, h 2½″. **511.** Santa Clara Pueblo. Minnie Vigil. Jar. d 4″. **512.** Santa Clara Pueblo. Minnie Vigil. Polychrome seed bowl. 1979. d 6½″, h 3⅛″. **513.** Santa Clara Pueblo. Minnie Vigil. Polychrome jar with feather design. 1977. d 2⅜″, h 2¼″. **514.** Santa Clara Pueblo. Minnie Vigil. Polychrome jar with feather design. 1976. d 3″, h 2¾″. **515.** Santa Clara Pueblo. Minnie Vigil. Polychrome seed bowl. 1978. d 4″.

516

517

518

519

520

521

Fig. 521 Courtesy Dave Ichelson

516. Santa Clara Pueblo. Minnie Vigil. Black-on-Red bowl. 1979. d 3⅛'', h 2⅛''.   **517.** Santa Clara Pueblo. Minnie Vigil. Black-on-Red, feather design seed bowl. 1979. d 3¾'', h 2¾''.   **518.** Santa Clara Pueblo. Minnie Vigil. Polychrome miniatures. 1977.   **519.** Santa Clara Pueblo. Minnie Vigil. Polychrome jar. 1979. d 5¼'', h 4½''.   **520.** Santa Clara Pueblo. Flora and Glenna Naranjo. Triangular bowl. 1975. d 3⅞'', h 2½''.   **521.** Santa Clara Pueblo. Carved black-ware. ca. 1975. d 5¼'', h 4¼''.

SAN ILDEFONSO

San Ildefonso Pueblo is known worldwide for the potters Julian and Maria Martinez and for its black-matte pottery.

Even those who only have a passing interest in Indian ceramics know of San Ildefonso black-matte pottery which has been associated with Julian and maria Martinez since about 1918.

Polished blackware has been made by most if not by all the Rio Grande Pueblos. At Pueblos such as Santa Clara, San Juan, Nambe, and San Ildefonso large, black, crudely-polished, thin-walled jars were used for water storage.

The Maria and Julian style of blackware differs from the former style of blackware by being thicker-walled, more finely polished with a gun metal black sheen, and unserviceable as a water container. Today the polished black pots from San Ildefonso and Santa Clara Pueblos share a continued highlight of popularity. Most of the pottery incorporates designs in black-matte of the avanyu or water serpent, feathers, simple geometric patterns or naturalistic symbols. Some, however, are plain without design. Plainware has been in continuous production since 1908. There are several families producing blackware at San Ildefonso.

Polychrome pottery also is being produced at San Ildefonso. Prior to recent popularity in polychrome pottery, there had been very little produced at San Ildefonso since 1920. Julian and Maria continued to make some polychrome until Julian's death in 1943 and most of these were unsigned (Peterson 1978). Today's San Ildefonso polychrome is aesthetically pleasing and for the most part represents experimentation, sometimes with very successful, appealing results. Since 1978 Carlos Dunlap has been making large polychrome, 12 to 24 inch diameter bowls. His feather designs and those of his mother, Carmelita Dunlap, are painted on a polished or textured rose-toned background. Execution of design is more bold with less attention to detail than the typical size pot. Dunlaps also continue to make polished blackware.

The Vigils—Albert, Josephine, Doug, and Charlotte, are making a thick-walled polished red-ware with traditional designs in white and cream tone. These are of high quality and are very pleasing.

The Martinez family represents a well known group of potters who are continuing to produce blackware. Three younger potters of this family, Pauline Martinez, Barbara Gonzales and Tony Da are known for contemporary forms in blackware.

These are executed with incising and burnishing techniques and frequently include the use of coral and turquoise.

Maria worked with clay in the family pottery-making room at San Ildefonso Pueblo until her death on July 20, 1980. Maria, who produced pottery during most of the 20th Century, used several forms of her name in signing her pots. The 1975 publication *Seven Families in Pueblo Pottery* by the Maxwell Museum of Anthropology provides a convenient listing of signatures accompanied by the approximate dates she used that signature. Maria was a very prolific potter and consequently her pottery is not rare. An approximate chronology of the signatures on Maria's pottery is as follows:

"Marie	Mid to late teens, 1934
Marie & Julian	1934-1943 (his death)
Marie & Santana	1943-1956
Maria and Popovi	1956-1971 (Popovi Da helped her in the late 40's and early 50's but did not paint for her until 1956).
Maria Poveka	Undecorated wares only (none prior to 1956)"[9]

Other members of the Maria Martinez family include Adam and Santana Martinez, Clara Montoya, Anita Martinez, and the Roybal family. Each is making outstanding pottery with a detectable uniqueness.

The practice of counterfeiting Maria's name on blackware has been reported; therefore, buyers should have a specialist examine the pot if there is doubt as to its authenticity. This procedure is not without flaws, but it is the only practical one. Several collectors have taken their pottery directly to San Ildefonso for identification.

There is some very inferior pottery produced at San Ildefonso as at other Pueblos. Fortunately, it is not abundant and its inferior quality is apparent even to the untrained eye. Examples might include poor polishing, cracks, or off-coloring.

There has been some crossover of blackware techniques and styles between San Ildefonso and Santa Clara. Generally, however, there are sufficient characteristics to distinguish blackware from these two Pueblos through shape, design, or tone of the polished black surface. But the best way to

[9] Maxwell Museum of Anthropology, 1974, *Seven Families in Pueblo Pottery*. The University of New Mexico. Albuquerque. p. 85.

distinguish between the two Pueblos is to study each potter and learn to identify each potter's style. Most quality blackware is signed by the potter today making identification definitive.

Rose Gonzales is another potter of fame at San Ildefonso. Born at San Juan Pueblo, she married Robert Gonzales of San Ildefonso in 1920. She learned ceramics at San Ildefonso and adopted her own style of polished blackware and redware. Although she makes black-matte pottery, she is identified with her beautiful black-polished carved pottery.

San Ildefonso Pueblo has a strong pottery tradition which is being carried forward by several young creative potters. Although there are relatively few potters at San Ildefonso, this Pueblo has made a significant contribution to the ceramic art.

523. San Ildefonso Pueblo. Marie and Julian Martinez. Polychrome olla. ca 1910. d 11½", h 11".

522. San Ildefonso Pueblo. ca 1916

Fig. 524, 527 Courtesy Fenn Galleries; 525 Courtesy Al Anthony; 528, 529 Courtesy Pueblo One

524. San Ildefonso Pueblo. Julian and Marie Martinez. ca 1920. h 10''.   **525.** San Ildefonso Pueblo. Marie and Santana. Fine black-matte olla. 1943-1956. d 7½'', h 7½''.   **526.** San Ildefonso Pueblo. Marie Martinez. Black-matte bowl, water serpent design. 1920-1934. d 9'', h 5½''.   **527.** San Ildefonso Pueblo. Marie and Santana. Black-matter jar. ca 1943-1956. h 4''.   **528.** San Ildefonso Pueblo. Polychrome bowl restored ca 1910. d 13'', h 6''.   **529.** San Ildefonso Pueblo. Polychrome olla, restored, ca 1910. d 13''.

Fig. 530, 531 Courtesy Pueblo One; 534, 535 Courtesy L. Blair

530. San Ildefonso Pueblo. Polychrome jar. Late 19th Century. d 11½'', h 9½''.　　　**531.** San Ildefonso Pueblo. Marie and Santana. Black-matte. 1943-1956. d 3¾'', h 3''.　　　**532.** San Ildefonso Pueblo. Marie and Santana Black-matte. 1943-1956. d 4'', h 3¼''.　　　**533.** San Ildefonso Pueblo. Marie and Santana. Black-matte, feather design. 1943-1956. d 3½'', h 2¾''.　　　**534.** San Ildefonso Pueblo. Marie. Vase with feather design, fair condition. ca 1928. d 6½'', h 6⅝''.　　　**535.** San Ildefonso Pueblo. Marie. Plate, black-matte with water serpent design, fair condition. ca 1928. d 13¼''.

Fig. 536 Courtesy Marguerite Kernaghan; 540 Courtesy Pueblo One; 541 Courtesy Nancy Daughters

536. San Ildefonso Pueblo. (Left) Marie and Julian. Black-matte wedding vase. 1934-1943. d 6'', h 7½''. (Center) Marie and Popovi also marked 633. Black-matte jar. 1962. This jar was presented as a gift to Marguerite Kernaghan by Popovi Da in 1963. d 9½'', h 7½''. (Right) Marie and Santana. Black-matte jar. 1943-1956. d 3½'', h 2½''. **537.** San Ildefonso Pueblo. Marie Poveka. Plain black polish bowl. 1979. d 5'', h 3¼''.   **538.** San Ildefonso Pueblo. Marie Poveka. Plain black polish bowl. 1979. d 3½'', h 2¾''.   **539.** San Ildefonso Pueblo. Marie Poveka. Plain black polish bowl. 1979. d 3⅜'', h 2¾''.   **540.** San Ildefonso Pueblo. Marie Poveka. Plain black polish bowl. ca 1956. d 5'', h 3''.   **541.** San Ildefonso Pueblo. Rose Gonzales. Wedding vase, award winner at 1979 Santa Fe Indian Market. 1979.. d 5½'', h 8⅝''.

167

Fig. 547 Courtesy Jerry & Dorothy Guinand

542. San Ildefonso Pueblo. Carlos Dunlap. Polychrome bowl. 1979. d 14'', h 9½''.　　**543.** San Ildefonso Pueblo. Carlos Dunlap. Polychrome with feather design bowl. 1979. d 8'', h 4¾''.　　**544.** San Ildefonso Pueblo. Carlos Dunlap. Polychrome bowl. 1979. d 5½'', h 4½''.　　**545.** San Ildefonso Pueblo. Carlos Dunlap. Polychrome bowl. 1979. d 5⅝'', h 4''.　　**546.** San Ildefonso Pueblo. Carlos Dunlap. Polychrome bowl. 1979. d 8¾'', h 5½''. **547.** San Ildefonso Pueblo. Carlos Dunlap. Polychrome bowl. 1977. d 8'', h 5''.

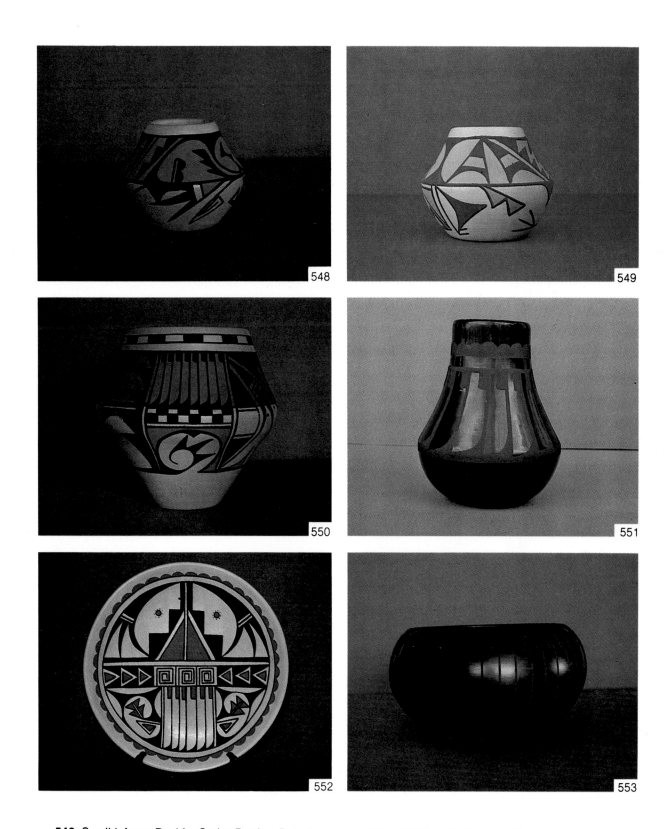

548. San Ildefonso Pueblo. Carlos Dunlap. Polychrome jar. 1979. d 5½'', h 4½''.   **549.** San Ildefonso Pueblo. Carlos Dunlap. Polychrome jar. 1979. d 5¾'', h 4½''.   **550.** San Ildefonso Pueblo. Carlos Dunlap. Polychrome jar. 1978. d 12'', h 11''.   **551.** San Ildefonso Pueblo. Carlos Dunlap. Black-matte vase. 1979. d 5'', h 5¾''. **552.** San Ildefonso Pueblo. Carmelita Dunlap. Polychrome plate. 1978. d 14''.   **553.** San Ildefonso Pueblo. Carmelita Dunlap. Black-matte feather bowl. 1979. d 11¾'', h 5¾''.

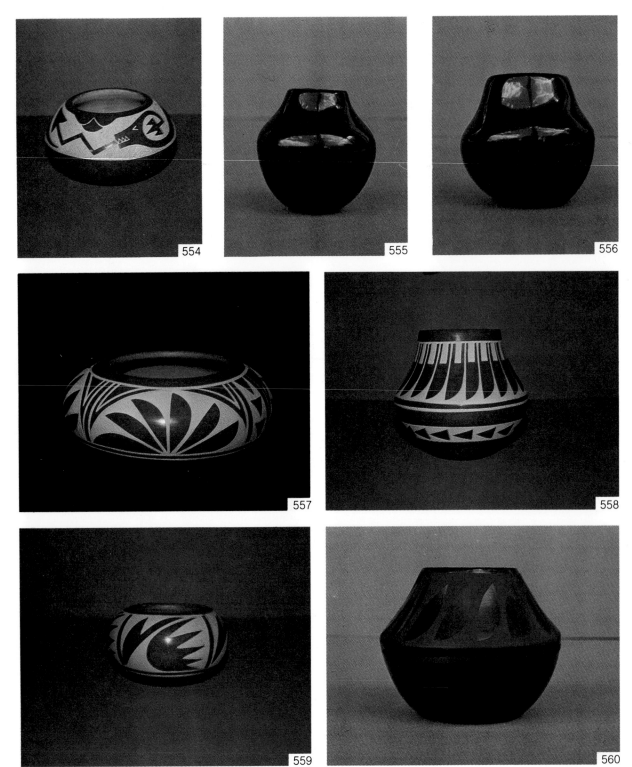

Fig. 554, 558, 559 Courtesy Nancy Daughters; 556, 557 Courtesy Indian Jewelry Center

554. San Ildefonso Pueblo. Adelphia. Water design incised on this red-polished bowl. 1976. d 4¾'', h 2½''. **555.** San Ildefonso Pueblo. Gregarita Baca. Black polish jar. 1977. d 2'', h 2''. **556.** San Ildefonso Pueblo. Gregarita Baca. Black polish jar. 1977. d 3'', h 2½''. **557.** San Ildefonso Pueblo. Albert and Josephine Vigil. Bow. 1978. d 7½'', h 3''. **558.** San Ildefonso Pueblo. Albert and Josephine Vigil. Vase. 1977. d 5½'', h 5''. **559.** San Ildefonso Pueblo. Albert and Josephine Vigil. Bowl. 1978. d 4¾'', h 2¾''. **560.** San Ildefonso Pueblo. Doug and Charlotte Vigil. Black-matte jar. 1979. d 4'', h 3''.

561. San Ildefonso Pueblo. Dora and Tse-Pe. Turtle with turquoise inlay. 1977. L 3''.　　**562.** San Ildefonso Pueblo. Blue Corn. (Left) Fine Polychrome jar. 1974. d 8½'', h 6½''. (Right) Seed jar. 1974. d 6¾'', h 4⅞''.　　**563.** San Ildefonso Pueblo. Blue Corn. Polychrome bowl. 1974. d 5⅜'', h 3⅛''.　　**564.** San Ildefonso Pueblo. (Left) Margaret Lou Gutierrez. Black-matte, feather design bowl. 1979. d 2½'', h 1½''. (Right) Blue Corn. Black-matte jar. 1970. d 2⅜'', h 1⅝''.　　**565.** San Ildefonso Pueblo. Barbara Gonzalez. Black and red burnished jar with stone inlay. 1978. d 3½'', h 3''.　　**566.** San Ildefonso Pueblo. Albert and Josephine Vigil. Jar with feather design. 1978.

SAN JUAN

The traditional pottery of San Juan Pueblo is a red slip on tan known as San Juan red-on-tan, and a black polished style jar. The latter is similar to the early blackware produced at Santa Clara. Most San Juan pottery shows evidence of a micaceous clay used in the slip which gives a slight glitter, similar to Taos and Picuris pottery.

The pottery revival at San Juan is evident today at the Pueblo's cooperative guild. A wide assortment of ceramics is available consisting of plain polished, polychromes of red, cream and tan, and a red incised style. The latter was developed by Regina Cata in 1930, and is being made today by several potters including Rosita Cata and Tomisita Montoya. San Juan's contemporary incised ware was inspired through observation of Potsuwi'i incised pottery sherds found at San Juan (Toulouse 1977). The new polychrome style which started in 1940 is particularly striking and clean with a contemporary flair. It is usually carved with geometric designs. Leonidas Tapia produced these fine polychromes in various styles until her death in the mid 1970's. Today, Rosita de Herrera is one of the outstanding producers of these fine polychrome pieces.

Tom Tapia is departing from San Juan tradition by making a style of polished blackware with incised designs. These fine pots, with detailed designs, are similar to the style developed by Joseph Lonewolf of the Santa Clara Pueblo. Tom Tapia's pots reveal orange within the incised field. This pottery is considered highly collectable.

Although there is relatively extensive pottery production at San Juan, their pottery is not common at Indian shops. As it becomes better known outside of New Mexico, demand will increase. San Juan pottery is an attractive addition to the contemporary decor.

567. San Juan Pueblo. ca 1915. Possibly Wesley Bradfield photo.

Courtesy San Diego Museum of Man, 3092.

568

569

570

571

572

573

Fig. 569 Courtesy Audrey Greenough

568. San Juan Pueblo. Leonidas Tapia. Fine example of modern San Juan Polychrome. 1974. d 5'', h 3½''. U.S. Army Photograph. **569.** San Juan Pueblo. Plate ca 1950. d 6¾''. **570.** San Juan Pueblo. Bowl. ca 1950. d 6½'', h 4½''. **571.** San Juan Pueblo. Leonidas Tapia. (Left) Wedding Vase. 1974. h 9½''. (Right) Rosita de Herrera. Bowl. 1976. d 6'', h 3⅜''. **572.** San Juan Pueblo. Rosita de Herrera. Bowl. 1976. d 6'', h 4''. **573.** San Juan Pueblo. Rosita de Herrera. Bowl. 1978. d 6'', h 4''.

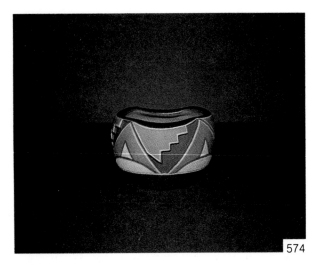

Fig. 574 Courtesy Nancy Daughters; 575, 576 Courtesy Dave Ichelson; 577, 578 Courtesy Bien Mur

574. San Juan Pueblo. Rosita de Herrera Bowl. 1977. d 5'', h 3⅜''. **575.** San Juan Pueblo. Tomisita Montoya. Incised bowl. ca 1970. d 5¼'', h 3½''. **576.** San Juan Pueblo. Blackware. ca 1900. (Left) d 4¼'', h 3''. (Right) d 3½'', h 3''. Dave Ichelson. **577.** San Juan Pueblo. Tom Tapia. 1979. (Left) incised jar. d 3½''. (Center) Incised jar. d 5¾'', h 6½''. (Right) Incised bow. d 3½'', h 2''. **578.** San Juan Pueblo. Tom Tapia. 1979. (Foreground) Incised eagle dancer, seed bowl. d 5'', h 2''. (Left) incised jar. d 4⅛'', h 3⅜''. (Center) h 2''. (Right) d 3¾'', h 3''.

TAOS AND PICURIS

A unique micaceous clay pottery is produced at the Pueblos of Taos and Picuris. Lack of participation by potters from these Pueblos at the 1979 and 1980 Santa Fe Indian Market suggests that their tradition is declining. One explanation of this decline is lack of customer interest. Today's collector looks for new creations and prefers either the highly-polished blackware produced at Santa Clara and San Ildefonso or the polychromes produced by several Pueblos. If an effort were undertaken to produce and market quality pottery at Taos and Picuris, in all probability collectors would welcome these pieces to their collections.

Mica, which is a component of their clay, serves as a ready tempering agent. After firing it takes on a golden sheen, although some pots are nearly black. This pottery can be particularly striking. Properly executed, adequately fired and seasoned, their lidded pots are excellent for baking. The famous "bean pot" of New Mexico was made at these Pueblos. A characteristic fire cloud is on most Taos and Picuris pottery. These are caused by the firing method. Decorations may consist of clay beading or fillets circumscribing the upper half or running along the rim. Handles and lids are placed on some pots. Virginia T. Romero of Taos and Virginia Duran of Picuris have been recognized for their high quality pots over the past decade. Alma Concha formerly of Taos made nativity sets in shades of red and tan. These are well executed and have a decided contemporary style.

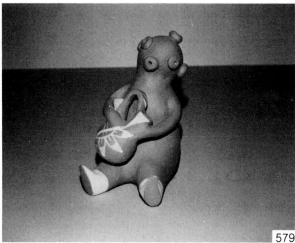

Courtesy Audrey Greenough. 579

Courtesy Pueblo One 580

Courtesy Pueblo Cultural Center and Museum of New Mexico. 581

579. Taos Pueblo. Alma L. Concha. Mud head figurine. ca 1975. h 5½''. Audrey Greenough Collection. **580.** Picuris Pueblo. Lucy Martiniz. Bowl. 1950. d 9½'', h 5¼''. **581.** Taos Pueblo. An assortment of 20th Century styles.

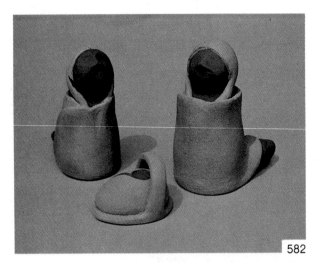

582

583

584

582. Taos. Alma Concha. Nativity set. 1977. h 4'',   **583.** Taos. Alma Concha. 1977. Approximately h 3''.
584. Taos. Virginia T. Romero. Bean pot. 1971. d 10'', h 6½''. Damaged.

SANDIA

Pottery was produced at Sandia Pueblo before 1900. By 1931 only one woman continued to produce pottery at Sandia (Sturtevant 1979). However, there have been recent attempts to produce pottery at San-dia. In 1978, I saw one bowl of recent origin, decorated red and black on cream bearing the Sandia mark. There were no Sandia pots marketed at San-dia's Bien Mur craft shop in 1979 or 1980.

ISLETA

Most Isleta pottery today is manufactured by non-traditional methods. Poster paint pottery production began at Isleta in the 1950's. A commercial white slip pottery decorated with Indian motifs in orange and dark brown currently is being made at Isleta. Such pottery is very popular with tourists because it is inexpensive and attractive.

Prior to 1950 there was some production of traditional pottery. Isleta potters made pottery called Isleta polychrome around the turn of the century for the tourist trade. Occasionally these polychrome pots turn up at auctions and flea markets in the Southwest where they are generally misidentified. Most pieces are simple bowls with dimensions up to 4 inches in diameter and 3 inches high. Twisted handles are not uncommon. This style of pottery reportedly was produced by Laguna people living near Isleta (Harlow 1977) around 1900. As might be expected, the techniques and designs on this pottery reveal a definite Laguna influence.

Today Stella Teller is an active Isleta potter. She makes a non-traditional ware with various Indian motif designs.

Courtesy Pueblo Cultural Center

Courtesy Barry Powell 586

587

588

585. Isleta Pueblo. ca 1880. Woman with olla. Photographer unknown. **586.** Isleta Pueblo. Tourist bowl, rare. ca 1900. d 4'', h 4''. **587.** Isleta Pueblo. Tourist bowl showing Laguna Pueblo influence. ca 1900. d 3½'', h 3''. **588.** Isleta Pueblo. Tourist bowl. ca 1900. d 4½'', h 3''.

589

590

Courtesy Pueblo Cultural Center

591

592

589. Isleta Pueblo. Tourist bowl. ca 1900. d 4½'', h 2''.   **590.** Isleta Pueblo. Stella Teller.   Wedding vase.
ca 1970. **591.** Isleta Pueblo. Stella Teller. Wedding vase. ca 1974. d 4½'', h 9''.   **592.** Isleta Pueblo. Stella Teller.
Polychrome bell. ca 1975. d 4''.

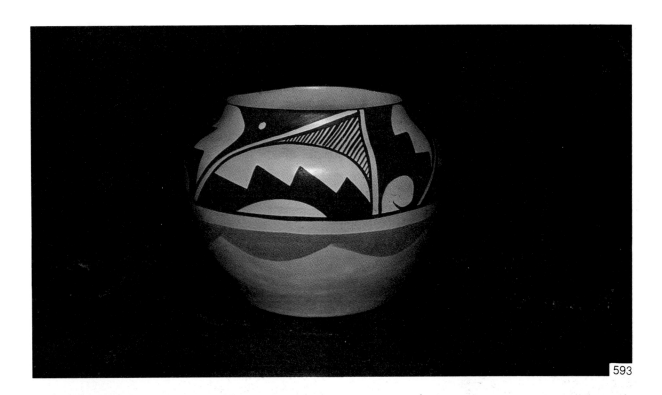

593

Courtesy Marguerite Kernaghan

594

593. Isleta Pueblo. Stella Teller. Polychrome jar. ca 1974. d 4'', h 5''.   **594.** Isleta Pueblo. Stella Teller. Polychrome bowl and vases. 1977-1979. (Left) d 5'', h 3½''. (Center) d 5½'', h 5½''. (Right) d 3½'', h 3''.

YSLETA-TIGUA

The Pueblo of Ysleta was founded in 1681 as a direct result of the Great Pueblo Revolt of 1680. Spanish soldiers and civilians took Isleta Pueblo people captive during the retreat southward. At the present site of El Paso, Texas, they established a village called Ysleta Del Sur. The present day Pueblo is small and has been continuously occupied since its establishment in 1681.

Little is known about Ysleta's historic pottery and no traditional pottery has been produced at Ysleta since the 1930's. In recent years potters have begun to produce a non-traditional style of pottery for the tourist market. They use either a potter's wheel or molds. Decorations consist primarily of geometric designs in black, white and orange on a textured orange base. Commerical paints are used and pots are fired in electric kilns. Prices range from a modest $2.50 to $75.00. Gloria Lujan and Lucy Rodela are active potters at Ysleta.

No collector pieces are produced; however, with their active marketing program it is conceiveable that potters will be motivated to advance their ceramic arts. It is doubtful that Ysleta will return to traditional methods of the pre 1930's.

595. Ysleta-Tigua. Lucy F. Rodela. Jar, made using modern ceramic methods. ca 1970. d 4¼", h 3¼".
596. Ysleta-Tigua. Lucy F. Rodela. Jar. d 8", h 6".

Courtesy Dave Ichelson

Fig. 596-602 Courtesy Bill Ciesla

597. Ysleta-Tigua. Lucy F. Rodela. Jar 1979. 5½'', h 3''.　　**598.** Ysleta-Tigua. Lucy F. Rodela. Vase 1979. d 2½'', h 4''.　　**599.** Ysleta-Tigua. Lucy F. Rodela. Wedding Vase. 1979. h 12''.　　**600.** Yselta-Tigua. Lucy F. Rodela. Jar. 1979. d 4½'', h 3''.　　**601.** Yselta-Tigua. Lucy F. Rodela. Jar. 1979. d 8'', h 5''.　　**602.** Yselta-Tigua. Potter unknown. Vase. 1978. d 5'', h 12''.

NAVAJO

The Navajo are relatively recent arrivals to the Southwest. They probably migrated from the north in the 16th Century thereby becoming a part of the Pueblo IV period.

The Navajo have made pottery since their arrival; possibly they brought pottery with them during their southern migration. They made a plain and decorated pottery, the plain being considered the older style. After the railroad's arrival to the Southwest in the 1880's, the Navajos reduced pottery production with the availability of commercially made utility ware at trading posts.

Today's Navajo pottery differs little from the old styles. It is often pear-shaped, conically-bottomed, and colored in a reddish brown. It is serviceable and made waterproof by coating with resin from piñon pine. Once the resin permeates the clay, the pot can be placed in hot coals with no loss of the resin or its sealing properties. Decorations are simple beading or applique. If the pot has the clay beads or fillets, a space or spirit break is included. It might appear as if the potter forgot to include one fillet. Anasazi culture potsherds are ground and used as a tempering agent. The pot is built by coiling, shaped by hand with the aid of a corn cob and fired in an open pit. Wedding vases and other vase styles are common. The Navajo has been known to make large jars but more commonly the pots are under 12 inches in height. The large jars are considered rare.

The Navajo people are probably the largest consumers of Navajo pottery. Therefore the Navajo potter makes pottery primarily for the Navajo trade. There is little collector demand at the present for Navajo pottery. This is somewhat unfortunate as it represents a definite style and is traditional in all aspects. Recently, however, several Navajo potters have been exhibiting and marketing pottery with various designs. Appliqued decorations representing yucca, cactus, horned toads, animals, humans, and flowers are appearing on their modern pottery. These have more appeal to collectors.

Alice Williams, Silas Claw, Stella Claw, Datso Bitsi, and the Tso family are active Navajo potters.[10]

They use their pottery for cooking, ceremonies, pipes, and drums, and do not consider it an art form. Public acceptance is not a motivation; in fact, the Navajo makes every effort to maintain privacy and anonymity. However, the Navajo are a large group and that leaves ample opportunity for exception to this social custom.

---

[10] Wright, H. Diane. 1980. Navajo Pottery Wins New Appreciation. In *The Indian Trader*, April 1980.

603

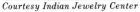
Courtesy Indian Jewelry Center

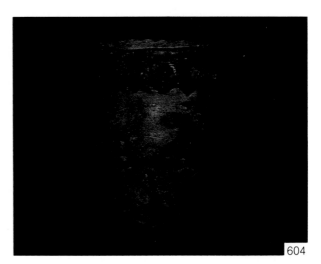

604

603. Navajo. Vase. 1978. d 2¾'', h 6''.

604. Navajo. Vase. 1973.

Fig. 605 Courtesy Bob LaPerriere; 606-609 Courtesy Indian Jewelry Center

605. Navajo. Vase. ca 1970. d 3½'', h 4''.   **606.** Navajo. Wedding Vase. 1975. d 6'', h 8½''. David Ichelson Collection.   **607.** Navajo. Vase. Note break on the right side of the filet design. This is a spirit break frequently seen on Navajo pots. ca 1960. d 4'', h 3⅝''.   **608.** Navajo. Vase. ca 1978. d 3½'', h 4¾''.   **609.** Navajo. Vase. ca 1978. d 2¼'', h 4¼''.

610

611

612

613

614

Fig. 610-614 Courtesy Indian Jewelry Center

610. Navajo. Pitcher. ca 1978. h 7''.   **611.** Navajo. Vase. 1977. d 4'', h 7½''.   **612.** Navajo. An assortment of shapes. ca 1978.   **613.** Navajo. Wedding Vase. 1977. d 3⅜'', h 4¾''.   **614.** Navajo. Wedding Vase. 1977. d 4'', h 7''.

184

615

616

617

618

619

620

Fig. 615 Courtesy Guinand Collection; 616, 617 Courtesy Indian Jewelry Center

615. Navajo. Wedding Vase. Handle cracked. ca 1960. h 9''.   **616.** Navajo. Vase. ca 1978. d 4½'', h 6''.
617. Navajo. Vase. ca 1977. d 4'', h 7½''.   **618.** Navajo. Pitcher. ca 1977. d 4¾'', h 7''.   **619.** Navajo. Vase.
ca 1973. d 4'', h 4¾''.   **620.** Navajo. Vase. ca 1973. d 5'', h 5''.

ZUNI

Zuni Pueblo is known today for its production of fine handcrafted jewelry. The technique of stone inlay and use of small turquoise and coral stones in all types of jewelry is highly prized by Indians and non-Indians the world over. Zuni jewelry tradition predates the Spaniards arrival. In prehistoric times, necklaces and bracelets were made of shell inlaid with turquoise. In 1965 there were approximately 900 Zunis silversmithing at the Pueblo (Sturtevant 1979), which suggests the importance of this industry at Zuni. Since the popularization of Indian jewelry during the early 1970's nearly every adult at Zuni has fashioned jewelry.

Historic (19th century) Zuni pottery also is highly prized by collectors who will pay premium prices for pieces even in fair condition. Prayer-meal bowls, ceremonial vessels, bird effigies, large jars, and food bowls were made during this period. Pottery drums were produced; however these are quite rare. The pottery was painted in red and black or brown with the latter used as bordering. Ceremonial breaks were placed in lines circling the vessel. As with Acoma pottery, a white slip is applied to the pot. The deer design, with a heartline, is common on Zuni pottery.

Decline in Zuni pottery production began around the beginning of the 19th century and culminated at the beginning of the 20th century.

Through the years, various individuals and institutions have tried to encourage the Zunis to revive pottery making. These attempts have not been successful for the reason that there must be Pueblo support and individuals with an interest in making pottery. Another factor was the demand for Zuni jewelry which was a better income producer than pottery.

During the 1970's when other Pueblos were reviving their pottery tradition, Zuni artists and craftsmen were busy attempting to fill all the orders for inlay and needle point jewelry.

Some pottery production has continued to the present. The Zuni owl is a popular tourist item, but even this is difficult to obtain. At the 1979 Santa Fe Indian Market only one potter, Jennie Laate, displayed Zuni pottery.

621. Zuni Pueblo. ca 1910.

622

623

624

Figure 622 Anschutz Collection; Courtesy Jane Du Bois; 623, 624 Courtesy Pueblo One

622. ''Zuni Pottery Maker'', oil, 20″ x 30″, 1907, W. R. Leigh. Anschutz Collection. Photo from the book *W. R. Leigh* by June Du Bois, p. 50.   **623.** Zuni Pueblo. Polychrome olla. Late 19th Century. h 10″. Richard M. Howard Collection. Photo courtesy Pueblo One.   **624.** Zia Pueblo. Polychrome bowl. Late 19th Century. d 14½″.

Fig. 625 Courtesy Pueblo One; 626, 627 Courtesy Fenn Galleries; 628, 630 Courtesy Pueblo One

625. Zuni Pueblo. Polychrome olla. rainbird design. 19th Century. h 12''. Eva Slater Collection.   **626.** Zuni Pueblo. Kiapkwa Polychrome. ca 1840. d 12'', h 9''.   **627.** Zuni Pueblo. Polychrome olla. ca 1840. d 12'', h 10''. **628.** Zuni Pueblo. Bowl. ca 1880. d 10½'', h 5½''.   **629.** Zuni Pueblo. Polychrome olla. ca 1900. d 13'', h 8½''. **630.** Zuni Pueblo. Polychrome olla. Late 19th Century.

Fig. 631 Courtesy Pueblo One; 632 Courtesy Don Bennett; 633, 634 Courtesy Pueblo Cultural Center and Museum of New Mexico; 635 Courtesy Marguerite Kernaghan

631. Zuni Pueblo. Polychrome olla. Late 19th Century. d 14'', h 10½''.　　**632.** Zuni Pueblo. Polychrome olla. Late 19th Century. Approximately d 11'', h 9½''.　　**633.** Zuni Pueblo. Polychrome bowl with appliqued frogs, probably pre-19th Century.　　**634.** Zuni Pueblo. Polychrome bowl with appliqued frogs. Date unknown, probably pre 19th Century.　　**635.** Zuni Pueblo. Polychrome olla. ca 1960. d 11'', h 9½''.　　**636.** Zuni Pueblo. Jennie Laate. Polychrome jar. 1979. d 3⅜'', h 4⅛''.

PAPAGO

The Papago relied upon large olla water jars for storage of water in their desert environment. Smaller vessels were made for other utilitarian purposes. The Papago habit was to cache pots containing water at stations located throughout their food gathering area. Often the cache would be beneath a ramada.

Papago pottery was made by the coil method with paddle and anvil. No slip was used and it was left either plain or decorated with simple whirls or spirals.

Although Papago potters made the largest ollas or jars associated with the historic Southwest, there has been relatively little collector interest. Perhaps the size of these ollas has been a deterrent. The Gila River Arts and Crafts Center near Scranton, Arizona, has several of these large ollas on exhibit in their museum.

Today several Papago potters make traditional pottery consisting of an undercoated polished brown ware, black-on-white, and a black-on-red similar to modern Maricopa pottery.

637

638

639

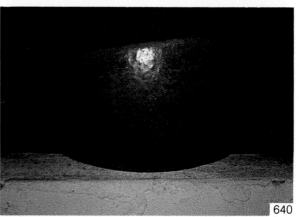
640

Fig. 637 Courtesy Public Archives of Canada; 638 Courtesy Pueblo One; 639 Courtesy Guinand Collection; 640 Courtesy Gila River Arts & Crafts

637. Papago potter using coil with paddle and anvil method of making pottery. The paddle is in her right hand while the stone anvil is in the foreground. Photo by Edward S. Curtis. In curtis, E. S. *The North American Indian* . . . (1908) Vo. 11, opp. p. 38.   **638.** Papago. Water jar. ca 1910, d 14'', h 17''.   **639.** Papago. Bowl with painted design. ca 1965. d 8½'', h 5½''.   **640.** Papago. Bowl with handles. ca 1979. d 8'', h 5''.

641

642

643

PIMA

The Pima made some pottery during the nine-teenth century; however little information is available on their pottery tradition.

644

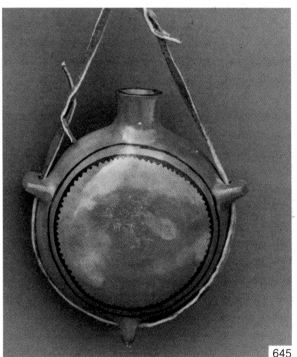

645

Fig. 641 Courtesy Jerry Mamola; 642 Courtesy Gila River Arts & Crafts; 643 Courtesy Dave Ichelson; 644, 645 Courtesy Bob LaPerriere

641. Papago. Decorated bowl. ca 1940. d 9'', h 6''. **642.** Papago. (Left) Lena Albert. Vase. 1979. d 4'', h 5''. (Center) Vase. 1979. d 4½'', h 5¼''. (Right) Vase. d 4'', h 4½''. **643.** Papago. Lena Albert. ca 1970. Fine effigy bowl. d 4½'', h 5''. **644.** Pima canteen. Late 19th Century. d 8''. (Damaged) **645.** Pima canteen. Late 19th Century. d 8''.

YUMAN GROUP

The Yuman, Maricopa, Cocopa, and Mojave made up the Colorado River Division of the Yuman Group. Of these tribes, the Mojave and Maricopa currently make pottery. Prehistoric Yuman pottery exceeded Pueblo pottery in thinness and hardness. Yuman and Pueblo pots were equal in symmetry but Yuman pottery lackled the high degree of painted decorations of the prehistoric Pueblo wares.

Mojave pottery is painted red on unslipped tan background similar to Hohokam pottery of prehistoric Arizona. As with the other desert cultures, the coil method, with paddle and anvil, was used to manufacture pottery. In decoration, Mojave pottery exceeded all other Yuman tribes both in quality and in production of painted ware.

Rogers (1973) indicated that demands of white purchasers in the 1880's were causing new pottery forms to appear and the indigenous ones to be discontinued. Tourist's partiality to figurines may have influenced the Mojave potter toward humanistic figures. The glass-beaded knick-knacks replaced their quality painted wares after 1900.

Yuman potters followed certain practices in regard to making and firing pottery. Fear of failure during firing of pottery caused potters to work in seclusion and to permit no one to see their pottery until it had been fired. I know of Pueblo potters today who follow this practice and have been told that the Navajo potters do likewise.

The Diegueno are part of the western division of the Yuman group. Present day members now live in southern California. No pottery has been made by this tribe or any other of the Yuman group in California since about 1965. There are, however, Diegueno people in California who retain the capability of making pottery.[11]

Annie Fields was one of the most famous modern Mojave potters. Before her death in the 1970's, she was actively producing a variety of humanistic figurines. These she decorated with beads and painted designs in red on a buff ceramic background. Her pottery is highly collectable. Occasionally a piece is available for sale at the Colorado River Indian Museum.

Colorado River Indian Reservation

Several potters are active at the Colorado River Indian Reservation, Parker, Arizona, representing several Southwestern tribes. During World War II some Pueblo people were translocated to this Reservation. Consequently, there is a variety of pottery styles being produced as each potter follows her tribal tradition. Ceramics classes are taught at the Reservation Museum.

Active potters include:
Estel Fisher - Hopi-Tewa
Madeline Zeyouma - Santa Clara Pueblo
Betty Gates - Mojave
Elmer Gates - Mojave
Amelia Asta
Francis Short

Colorado River Indian ceramics are available for purchase at the Museum.

Maricopa

The Maricopa of Arizona today produce a black-on-red and a black-on-white pottery. The black-on-red is more common. Black designs are painted on a highly polished red surface after firing. The black paint may be commercial or a thickened mesquite juice. Firing is by electric kiln or the traditional firing pit. Besides painted designs, figures of human or lizards may be incorporated by molding or applique. Bowls, wedding vases, and long necked vases are characteristic of maricopa pottery. An assortment of Maricopa pots are on display at Gila River Arts and Crafts Center near Scranton, Arizona.

Table 4. Styles and public prices of pottery made by Elmer Gates, Mojave Tribe. Source is Colorado River Reservation, May 1980, at the Reservation Museum, Parker, AZ.

STYLE	PRICES	STYLE	PRICES
TWO FACE EFFIGY	$ 55.00/60.00	OWLS	$ 25.00
FROGS	25.00	WEDDING JUG	65.00
TWIN POTS	50.00	PAIR LARGE DOLLS	110.00
SITTING DOLLS	55.00 Pair	LARGE TWIN POT	95.00
STANDING DOLLS	55.00 Pair	LARGE EFFIGY POT	100.00
LARGE DOLLS	55.00	EFFIGY BOWLS	45.00
BOWLS	12.00/15.00	VASE	20.00
ONE FACE EFFIGY	45.00	SINGLE HEADED EFFIGY	75.00
SNAKE POT	45.00	DOUBLE HEAD EFFIGY	150.00
PIGS	45.00	TWIN HEADED EFFIGY POT	65.00
TURTLES	20.00	RAG DOLLS	15.00

[11]Personal communications, Dr. Kenneth Hedges, San Diego Museum of Man, May 1980.

646

647

648

649

650

651

646. Maricopa potter. 1919.   **647.** Maricopa. (Left) ca 1950. d 3½''. (Right) ca 1950. d 3''. Audrey Greenough Collection.   **648.** Maricopa. Vesta Breed. Bowl with applliqued serpent design. ca 1965. d 5½'', h 3¼''. **649.** Maricopa. Mary Juan. Fine bowl. ca 1970. d 6'', h 2½''.   **650.** Maricopa. Phyllis Johnson. Wedding vase. ca 1965. h 5½''.   **651.** Maricopa. (Left) Vase. ca 1940. d 3'', h 3½''. (Right) Bowl. ca 1940. d 5½'', h 4''.

652

653

654

655

Fig. 652 Courtesy Gila River Arts & Crafts; 653-655 Courtesy Dave Ichelson

652. Maricopa. An assortment of modern (1979) pots ranging from 4'' to 16''. Large vase in center was made by Barbara Johnson, h 16''.　　**653.** Maricopa. Jar. ca 1960. d 5½'', h 5''.　　**654.** Maricopa. Vase. ca 1950. d 3'', h 3½''.　　**655.** Maricopa. Bowl. ca 1950. d 5½'', h 5½''.

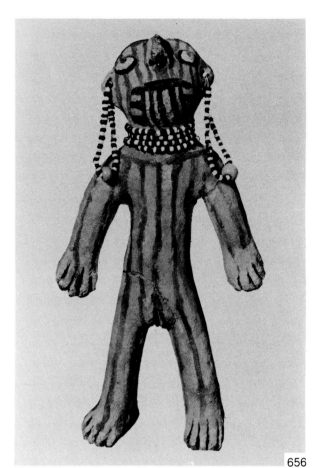

656

657

658

Fig. 656 Courtesy San Diego Museum of Man; 657, 658 Courtesy Jerry Mamola

656. Mojave. Clay doll. Historic Period.   **657.** Mojave. Anne Fields. ca 1960. d 6″, h 7″.   **658.** Mojave. Cup and saucer with Hohokam design, damaged. d 6″, h 5″.

CATAWBA

Pottery provided the chief support of the Catawba tribe in 1908 (Harrington 1908). It was the occupation of nearly every Catawba household. Of all the eastern tribes, the Catawba were the most active potters.

A small tribe located at Rock Hill, South Carolina, they were known for their high-quality pottery, and consequently their pottery was in demand by the early settlers. Influenced by white man's ceramics, Catawba potters produced tradeware in the form of vases, pitchers, and flower pots. This tableware did not exhibit Indian character in design or form.

Catawba potters always have practiced the traditional coil method and open pit firing to make their pottery. Scraping and polishing were done in a similar fashion practiced by Pueblo potters. Of interest is the firing method of producing blackware which as described by Harrington (1908) is nearly identical to that of the San Ildefonso Pueblo.

Today, two Catawba women are producing traditional pottery. Sara Ayers at West Columbia, South Carolina, and Francis Wade of Rock Hill, South Carolina, make a variety of styles including vases, bowls, cups, and pitchers.

There are several potters at the Catawba Indian Craftsmen's Association at Rock Hill, South Carolina. Georgia Harris is one of these potters. She learned pottery making from her grandmother, Martha Jane Harris, who was recognized by white settlers for her fine pottery. Georgia Harris makes effigy bowls which have always been a preferred style with the Catawba. She had a one-person show in 1977, sponsored in part by the U.S. Department of Interior's Indian Arts and Crafts Board.

Today Catawba potters still covet their clay deposits and it is rare that an outsider is permitted entry to the clay pits.

659. Catawba. Sara Lee Ayers. Effigy jar. 1971. h 9-3/8".

Courtesy U.S. Dept of Interior—Indian Arts & Crafts Board WD 72.73

CHEROKEE

The present day Cherokee represents one of the last vestiges of native ceramic production in the eastern United States. Prehistorically, pottery was produced by nearly all the major tribal units in central and eastern United States. Today, only a few groups produce traditional pottery.

Several Cherokee potters have distinguished themselves in the ceramic arts producing both traditional and contemporary innovations.

Cherokee potters are active near Tahlequah, Oklahoma, and at Cherokee, North Carolina.

Anna B. Mitchel has been making pottery since 1969 when she discovered red, yellow and gray clay on her property. An interest was aroused and she wanted to prove to herself that she could make pottery following traditional methods. She and her husband, Robert, researched methods of making and decorating pottery following in the Southeastern Woodlands Indian tradition. Through persistence and trial and error, Anna Mitchel rediscovered the "old" method. She uses a grinding stone to pulverize the clay; a smooth rock for polishing; wooden paddles for shaping; cane reeds, turkey bones, and twigs for decorating; the gray, red, and yellow clay for slip; and a primitive outdoor kiln. She produces a variety of pottery styles: urns, vases, and bowls which retail from $60 to $500. She decorates her pottery with incised swirling patterns.

Cora Wahnetah has been making pottery for over 45 years near Cherokee, North Carolina. Her technique follows strictly the old method of coiling and in the case of effigy pieces, by modeling. She is noted for her fine incised designs and for her distinguished dark and evanescent wood-smoked finishes which she achieves by open pit firing.

Other Cherokee potters have established themselves in recent years as ceramists but have modernized the techniques by use of the potter's wheel, commercial clay, and use of electric kiln.

Cherokee potters in Oklahoma market their pottery primarily at the Cherokee Arts and Crafts Center, Tahlequah, Oklahoma, and the eastern Cherokee potters market their pottery at the Qualla Arts and Crafts Mutual, Cherokee, North Carolina.

660. Cherokee. Cora Wahnetah. Effigy bowl. 1968. h 6-3/8", l 9½".

Courtesy U.S. Dept of Interior—Indian Arts & Crafts Board W.H. 69.41.2

197

661

662

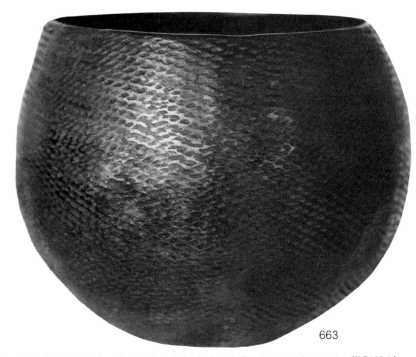

663

Fig. 661-663 Courtesy U.S. Dept of Interior—Indian Arts & Crafts Board, WD 75.13.1; AB 1279. A1; W-B198.1A.

661. Cherokee. Louise Bigmeat Maney. Lidded jar. 1975. h 8''. **662.** Cherokee. Anna B. Mitchell. Owl effigy jar. 1977. h 6''. **663.** Cherokee. Cora Wahnetah. 1965. h 6¾''.

COUSHATTA

Coushatta or Koasati of southern Louisiana make a traditional pottery. Firing in the same manner as the outdoor fire pit method used by the Pueblo potters, their pottery is polished and designs applied by incising before firing. They make an orange and sometimes a blackware.

In 1977, their pottery was priced up to $100.00 retail.

The Langley family, Rosalane, Ronald, Paul and Lorna are known to produce pottery today. Located at the Coushatta Reservation, Elton, Louisiana, they produce only a small amount of pottery for special orders or for gifts. Their pottery is still made in the traditional manner, etched or incised and polished before firing.

PAMUNKEY

The Pamunkey tribe markets pottery at their Reservation trading post located approximately 22 miles northeast of Richmond, Virginia.

Approximately six potters practice the traditional methods of making pottery. Pocahontas Cook, who lives on the Reservation, reported that Pamunkey potters use a grey clay which they collect locally[12]. When fired in an electric kiln, the clay turns red and when fired outdoors in a pit the clay turns black. Polishing is accomplished by rubbing the surface with a piece of deer antler or a smooth stone. Their pottery either is incised or plain. Mrs. Cook indicated that there is some non-traditional glazed pottery also being made by Pamunkey Indians. It is unknown to what extent glazed pottery is being made at the Reservation.

---

[12]Personal communication with Pocahontas Cook, May 1980.

Table 5 - General characteristics of contemporary pottery produced today, by Pueblo: X = characteristic; P = possible.

CHARACTERISTIC	Acoma	Cochiti	Hopi	Isleta	Jemez	Laguna	Nambe	Pojoaque	Picuris	San Juan	San Felipe	San Ildefonso	Sandia	Santa Ana	Santa Clara	Santo Domingo	Taos	Tesuque	Zia	Zuni
Red polish undecorated			X		X		X	X		X		X		X	X					
Black polish							X	X	P			X		X	X		P			
Black matte												X		X						
Red polish-matte					X		X			X		X		X	X					
Black on white	X	X	X	P	P	X		X						X		X				
White on red					X		X	X		X		X		X						
Polychrome	X	X	X	X	X	X	X	X	X	X	P	X	P	X	X	X		X	X	X
Carved							X			X		X		X						
Incised			X							X		X		X						
Corrugated	X		X																	
Floral design	X	P				X						X		X		X				
Bird design	X	X	X		X	X				X				P		X	X		X	X
Animal design	X	X					X	X						X			X		X	X
Bear paw design								X						X						
Water serpent							X	X				X		X						
Feather design					X		X	X				X		X						
Geometric design	X		X	X	X	X	X	X		X				X	X	X	X		X	X
Nativity scenes		X			X									X		X				
Storytellers	X	X		P	X									X		X	X			
Spirit break		X		P	P						X		X		X		X	P	X	
Utilitarian	X	X	P			P			X					X	X	X		X		
Micaceous clay							X		X	X					P		X			
Poster paints																X				
Acrylic paints			X	X													P	X		
Traditional paints	X	X	X		X	X	X	X		X	X	X	P	X	X	X		X	X	X
Thin wall	X																		X	
Traditional firing	X	X	X		X	X	X	X	X	X	X	X		X	X	X	X	X	X	X
Electric kiln use	P		X	X	P											P		P	P	
Traditional	X	X	X		P	X	X	X	X	X	X	X	P	X	X	X	X	X	X	X
Non-traditional				X	X											X	X	X		
Limited production				X		X	X	X	X	X			P	X	X	X	X		X	

200

VI

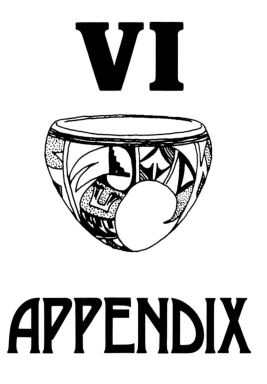

APPENDIX

GLOSSARY

Following are definitions as used within the context of this book.

Appliques — Practice of affixing figures, such as animals and corn to surface of pottery by potters at Jemez, San Felipe, Cochiti, etc.

Avanyu — A serpent design on Pueblo pottery especially from San Ildefonso and Santa Clara Pueblos; also referred to as water serpent, feathered water serpent and horned serpent. Reportedly represents water.

Bearpaw design — Found on some Santa Clara Pueblo traditional pottery represented as an imprint.

Black-on-black — A type of blackware pottery finished both by black polish and dull or matte finish usually suggesting a design. Also called black-matte pottery.

Carved — Deep depressions carved in pottery before firing; characteristic of some Santa Clara pottery.

Blackware — Any type of black pottery, plain, carved, polished or decorated, made primarily at Santa Clara and San Ildefonso Pueblos. Red clay used to make blackware turns black from carbon released during low temperature and reduced oxygen atmosphere.

Ceremonial break — An interruption or break in a design which circles the pot. Characteristic on traditional pottery from San Felipe, Santo Domingo, Cochiti and the Navajo tribe. Some prehistoric pottery such as Pecos Glaze V also had a ceremonial break. Also called a spirit break.

Collector — Persons and institutions who have an appreciation for Indian ceramics and who share a responsibility for providing incentives to the artist to continue in pursuit of ceramics.

Crazing — Discontinuity or fine cracks in the slip possibly due to uneven shrinkage of the underlying clay.

Facets — Lines or faint grooves remaining in a polished surface — the fewer the facets, the better the polish.

Fillet — An applique banding circling the pot. It is made of the same clay used to make the pot. Characteristic of decorations on Navajo pottery.

Fire cloud — Blemish on a pot caused by pot coming in contact with a piece of fuel, thus being fired at a higher temperature

Historic pottery — Pottery produced after the arrival and influence of Europeans to North America and continuing to the beginning of the 20th century.

Incised — Design placed on pot, before or after firing, by a pointed tool which removes the slip and exposes the underlying clay.

Micaceous clay — Clay containing mica; characteristically used by potters at San Juan, Taos, and Picuris.

Mineral paint — Paint made from inorganic compounds such as iron and usually mixed with vegetal base materials.

Modern or contemporary pottery — Pottery produced after 1900 - 1930 by pottery-producing tribes and Pueblos.

Non-traditional — Pottery made by other than traditional methods such as potter's wheel, electric kiln firing use of commercial

	paints, etc. Some pottery is made using a combination of traditional and non-traditional methods.	Temper	A non-plastic additive to the clay which counteracts shrinkage and facilitates uniform drying, thus allowing for more even cooling and heating during firing. This reduces the chance of breakage which would otherwise occur because of uneven pressures. Sand, volcanic rock and potsherds are used as a tempering agent.
Olla	Large pot used as a water container.		
Pitting	Problem observed occasionally on Pueblo pottery resulting from expansion and contraction of improperly prepared clay or impure clay. Also referred to as "spall off". Evident as small, 1 to 2 mm diameter pits on finished surface which exposes underlying material.		
		Tradeware	Pottery produced primarily for trade purposes. Several of the prehistoric groups produced trade pottery, and by definition almost all pottery produced today may be referred to as trade ware.
Polishing	Procedure used to achieve a polished surface on pot by rubbing with a smooth stone, leather or cloth.		
		Traditional pottery	Pottery produced by following ancient ways, i.e. coiling, use of native paints, and fired in an outdoor pit. These pots usually are similar to early shapes and designs.
Polychrome	Pottery with three or more colors or tones, making up the color scheme.		
Prehistoric pottery	Pottery produced prior to the arrival of Europeans in North America.		
Redware	Red pottery primarily at Santa Clara and San Ildefonso Pueblos. Made with same clay as used in blackware.	Tourist	Casual visitor who may purchase inexpensive pottery as a curio or souvenir.
		Tourist pot	Pottery produced primarily for the tourist trade, also referred to as curio, souvenir, or knick-knack.
Rocky Mountain bee plant	*Cleome serrulata* Pursh: a plant which is boiled to obtain black paint, also called wild spinach or quelites. Boiled product also called guaco.		
		Utility ware	Term applied to pottery used for everyday needs such as cooking, eating and storage. This term is commonly used by archaeologists to describe pottery which is not decorated except for indentations, and was used for cooking, storage, etc.
Seed bowl	Pot with small opening representing a former use by the Pueblo for seed storage.		
Sherd or shard	Broken pieces of pottery sometimes ground and used as a temper in the clay mixture; also called a potsherd.		
Slip	Coating of watered-down clay applied to the surface of a pot before firing. The slip may be polished or left as a matte finish.	Vegetal paint	Paint made from native plants such as Rocky Mountain bee plant, mustard and wild spinach, sometimes mixed with minerals.

SOURCES AND SELECTED REFERENCES

Following is a list of publications which have been referred to in preparation of this book. The list is only a few of the publications on North American Indian pottery. For those who wish to pursue various subjects this list will be a beginning.

Arizona Highways. 1974.
Special Prehistoric Pottery Issue. February 1974, Vol. L. No. 2. Phoenix.

Arizona Highways. 1974.
Special Edition Southwestern Pottery Today. May 1974, Vol. L No. 5. Phoenix.

Bartlett, Katharine. 1977.
A History of Hopi Pottery. *Plateau*, 49(3):2-13. Museum of Northern Arizona: Flagstaff.

Boyle, David. 1895.
Notes on Primitive Man in Ontario. An Appendix to the Report of the Minister of Education for Ontario. Toronto: Warwick Bros. & Rutter, Printers.

Bryant, Keith L., Jr. 1974.
History of the Atchison, Topeka and Santa Fe Railway. New York and London: Macmillan Pub. Co.

Bunzel, Ruth L. 1929.
The Pueblo Potter. Columbia University Contributions to Anthropology 8:1-134. Reprinted 1972 by Dover Publications, New York.

Ceram, C. W. 1972.
The First American. New York and Scarborough: New American Library.

Chapman, Kenneth. 1939.
The Pottery of Santo Domingo. *Laboratory of Anthropology Memoir* 1. Santa Fe.

Chapman, Kenneth. 1970.
The Pottery of San Ildefonso Pueblo. School of American Research. Monograph Series, No. 28. Alburquerque: University of New Mexico Press.

Collins, John E. 1975.
A Tribute to Lucy M. Lewis. Museum of North Orange County. Fullerton, Calif.

Colton, Harold S. 1953.
Potsherds, An Introduction to the Study of Prehistoric Southwestern Ceramics and Their Use in Historic Reconstruction. *Museum of Northern Arizona Bulletin* 25. Flagstaff.

Cushing, F. H. 1886.
A Study of Pueblo Pottery as Illustrative of Zuni Culture Growth. In *4th Annual Report of the Bureau of Ethnology for the Years 1882-1883.* Washington.

Dedera, Don. 1973.
In Praise of Pueblo Potters. *EXXON USA XII* (2):1-8. Houston.

DuBois, June. 1977.
W. R. Leigh. Kansas City: The Lowell Press.

Fowler, William S. 1966.
Ceremonial and Domestic Products of Aboriginal New England. Bulletin of the Massachusetts Archaeological Society, 27(3-4):51-61. Attleboro.

Frank, Harry and Francis H. Harlow. 1974.
Historic Pottery of the Pueblo Indians. New York Graphic Society: Boston.

Goddard, Pliny Earle. 1928.
Pottery of the Southwestern Indians. The American Museum of Natural History. New York.

Harlow, Francis H. 1970.
Historic Pueblo Indian Pottery. Santa Fe: Museum of New Mexico Press.

Harlow, Francis H. 1973.
Matte Paint Pottery of the Tewa, Keres and Zuni Pueblos. Santa Fe: Museum of New Mexico Press.

Harlow, Francis H. 1977.
Modern Pueblo Pottery. Flagstaff: Northland Press.

Harrington, M. R. 1908.
Catawba Potters and Their Work. *American Anthropologist* 10(3):399-407.

Heizer, R. F., and M. A. Whipple, eds. 1970.
The California Indians. Berkeley and Los Angeles: University of California Press.

Hewett, Edgar L. 1906.
Antiquities of the Jemez Plateau, New Mexico. *Bureau of American Ethnology Bulletin* 32. Washington.

Hitchcock, Ann. 1977.
A Consumer's Guide to Hopi Pottery. *Plateau,* 49(3):22-31, Museum of Northern Arizona. Flagstaff.

Holmes, William. H. 1886.
Pottery of the Ancient Pueblos. In *4th Annual Report of the Bureau of Ethnology for the Years 1882-1883.* Washington.

Hothem, Lar. 1984.
North American Indian Artifacts. Florence, Alabama: Books Americana.

Howard, Richard M. 1968.
The Mesa Verde Musuem. Flagstaff: KC Publications.

Hyde, Hazel. 1973.
Maria Making Pottery. Santa Fe: Sunstone Press.

Kessel, John L. 1979.
Kiva, Cross, and Crown. U.S. Department of the Interior, National Park Service. Washington.

Kidder, Alfred Vincent. 1963.
An Introduction to the Study of Southwestern Archaeology. 2nd ed. With a preliminary account of the excavations at Pecos and a summary of Southwestern archaeology today by Irving Rouse. New Haven and London: Yale University Press.

Lambert, Marjorie F. 1966.
Pueblo Indian Pottery: Materials, Tools, and Techniques. Santa Fe: Museum of New Mexico Press.

Le Free, Betty. 1975.
Santa Clara Pueblo Pottery. School of American Research. Monograph Series No. 29. Albuquerque: University of New Mexico Press.

Marriott, Alice. 1948.
Maria: The Potter of San Ildefonso. Norman: University of Oklahoma Press.

Martin, Paul S., George I. Quimby, and Donald Martin. 1947.
Indians Before Columbus. Chicago and London: The University of Chicago Press.

Massachusetts Archaeological Society. 1977.
A Handbook of Indian Artifacts from Southern New England. Bronson Museum. Attleboro, Mass.

Maxwell Museum of Anthropology. 1974.
Seven Families in Pueblo Pottery. Albuquerque: University of New Mexico Press.

Monthan, Guy, and Doris Monthan. 1979.
Nacimientos. Flagstaff: Northland Press.

Peterson, Susan. 1977.
The Living Tradition of Maria Martinez. Tokyo, New York and San Francisco: Kodansha International.

Peterson, Susan. 1978.
    Maria Martinez—Five Generations of Potters. Renwick Gallery of the National
    Collection of Fine Arts. Washington: Smithsonian Institution Press.

Pilles, Peter J., Jr. 1974.
    The Prehistory of Pottery of Arizona. In Arizona Highways, Vol. L (2).
    Phoenix.

Prufer, Olaf H. 1964.
    Ohio Hopewell Ceramics: An Analysis of the Extant Collection. *University of
    Michigan Museum of Anthropology, Anthropological Paper* 33. Ann Arbor.

Reiter, Paul. 1938.
    The Jemez Pueblo of Unshagi, New Mexico Part 1. *A Monograph of the Univer-
    sity of New Mexico and the School of American Research, No. 5.* Santa Fe.

Rivard, Jean-Jacques, ed. 1976.
    A Handbook of Indian Artifacts from Southern New England. The
    Massachusetts Archaeological Society. Attleboro.

Roberts, Frank H. H., Jr. 1932.
    The Villages of the Great Kivas on the Zuni Reservation New Mexico. *Bureau of
    American Ethnology Bulletin* 111. Washington.

Rogers, Malcolm J. 1936.
    Yuman Pottery Making. In *San Diego Museum Papers No. 2*, pp. 52. Reprinted
    1973 by Ballena Press. Romona, CA.

Shetrone, H. C. 1951.
    Primer of Ohio Archaeology, 5th edition. The Ohio State Archaeological and
    Historical Society. Columbus.

Spivey, Richard L. 1979.
    Maria. Flagstaff: Northland Press.

Stanislawski, Michael B., Ann Hitchcock, and Barbara B. Stanislawski. 1976.
    Identification Marks on Hopi and Hopi-Tewa Pottery. *Plateau*, 48(3,4):47-65.
    Quarterly of the Museum of Northern Arizona, Flagstaff.

Sturtevant, William C., and Robert F. Heizer, eds. 1978.
    Handbook of North American Indians, Vol. 8 California. Smithsonian Institu-
    tion. Washington.

Sturtevant, William C., and Bruce G. Trigger, eds. 1978.
    Handbook of North American Indians, Vol. 15 Northeast. Smithsonian Institu-
    tion. Washington.

Sturtevant, William C., and Alfonso Ortiz, eds. 1979.
    Handbook of North American Indians. Vol. 9 Southwest. Smithsonian
    Institution, Washington.

Tanner, Clara Lee. 1968.
    Southwest Indian Craft Arts. Tucson: University of Arizona Press.

Tanner, Clara Lee. 1976.
    Prehistoric Southwestern Craft Arts. Tucson: University of Arizona Press.

Toulouse, Betty. 1977.
    Pueblo Pottery of the New Mexico Indians. Santa Fe: Museum of New Mexico
    Press.

Tryk, Sheila. 1979.
    Solving the Pecos Pottery Mystery. *New Mexico Magazine* 57(7):20-23. Santa
    Fe.

Underhill, Ruth. 1944.
    Pueblo Crafts. U.S. Department of the Interior, Bureau of Indian Affairs.
    Washington.

White, Leslie A. 1962.
    The Pueblo of Sia, New Mexico *Bureau of American Ethnology Bulletin* 184.
    Washington.

Wormington, H. M. 1947.
Prehistoric Indians of the Southwest. The Denver Museum of Natural History. Denver.

Wormington, H. M., and Arminta Neal. 1974.
The Story of Pueblo Pottery, 4th edition. The Denver Museum of Natural History. Denver.

POTTERY COLLECTIONS

Following is a partial list of private and public institutions which have major collections of North American Indian pottery. Primarily each institution specializes in pottery of its respective geographic area or region. Some, however, have expanded their collections of pottery with representative types of several North American cultures. The Milwaukee Public Museum and the Smithsonian Institute are two examples of the latter. Additionally, fine collections of prehistoric pottery are on exhibit at most National Monuments and National Parks located at archaeological sites.

Arizona State Museum
University of Arizona
Tucson, AR 85721

Bronson Museum
8 North Main Street
Attleboro, MA 02703

Cherokee National Historical Society, Inc.
P.O. Box 515
Tahlequah, OK 94464

Colorado River Indian Reservation Museum
Parker, AZ 85344

Denver Art Museum
100 West 14th Avenue Parkway
Denver, CO 80204

Denver Museum of Natural History
City Park
Denver, CO 80205

El Pueblo Museum
905 S. Prairie Avenue
Pueblo, CO 81005

Field Museum of Natural History
Roosevelt Road at
Lake Shore Drive
Chicago, IL 60605

Heard Museum
22 E. Monte Vista Road
Phoenix, AZ 85004

Illinois State Museum
Spring and Edwards
Springfield, IL 62706

Institute of American Indian Arts Museum
Cerrillos Road
Santa Fe, NM 87501

Kit Carson Memorial Foundation, Inc.
Old Kit Carson Road
Taos, NM 87571

Maxwell Museum of Anthropology
Roma and University, N.E.
Albuquerque, NM 87131

Milwaukee Public Museum
800 West Wells Street
Milwaukee, WI 53233

Museum of Anthropology
Lafferty Hall
University of Kentucky
Lexington, KY 40506

Museum of Anthropology
University of Kansas
Lawrence, KS 66044

Museum of Anthropology
University of Missouri
100 Swallow Hall
Columbia, MO 65201

Museum of Big Bend
Sul Ross State University
Alpine, TX 79830

Museum of Man
Wake Forest University
106 Reynolda Village
Winston-Salem, NC 27106

Museum of New Mexico
P.O. Box 2087
Santa Fe, NM 87501

Museum of Northern Arizona
Fort Valley Road
Flagstaff, AZ 86001

Museum of Science and History
McArthur Park
Little Rock, AR 72202

Museum of the American Indian
Heye Foundation
Broadway at 155th Street
New York City, NY 10032

Museum
University of Colorado at Boulder
Boulder, CO 80309

National Museum of Canada
300 Laurier Avenue West
Ottawa, Ontario KIA OM8
Canada

Nebraska State Historical Society
1500 R Street
Lincoln, NE 68508

Ohio Historical Society
Interstate 71 and 17th Avenue
Columbus, OH 43211

Peabody Museum of Archaeology and Ethnology
11 Divinity Avenue
Cambridge, MA 02138

Reading Public Museum and Art Gallery
500 Museum Road
Reading, PA 19611

Robert S. Peabody Foundation for Archaeology
Corner of Phillips and
Main Street
Andover, MA 01810

San Diego Museum of Man
1350 El Prado, Balboa Park
San Diego, CA 92101

Southwest Museum
234 Museum Drive
Los Angeles, CA 92101

Texas Memorial Museum
2400 Trinity
Austin, TX 78705

Thomas Gilcrease Institute of American History and Art
1400 North 25 West Avenue
Tulsa, OK 74127

Utah Museum of Natural History
University of Utah
Salt Lake City, UT 84112

Western New Mexico University Museum
Box 43
Silver City, NM 88061

Wheelwright Museum
704 Camino Lejo
Santa Fe, NM 87501

INDEX

PRICING INDEX

Figure	Value ($)	Figure	Value ($)	Figure	Value ($)	Figure	Value ($)
1-130	——	184	150	245 (L)	375	290	75
131	700	185	250	245 (C)	125	291	80
132	600	186	800	245 (R)	300	292	100-800
133	750	187	375	246 (L)	150	293	750
134	75	188	350	246 (C)	60	294 (L)	225
135-136	950	189	375	246 (R)	175	294 (R)	400
137	850	190	450	247	150	295	175
138	550	191	575	248 (T)	700	296	175
139 (L)	575	192	550	248 (B)	400	297	95
139 (R)	875	193	500	249 (L)	300	298	375
140	300	194	200	249 (R)	500	299	375
141	600	195 (L)	150	250	75	300-303	——
142	300	195 (R)	250	251 (L)	500	304 (L)	40
143	500	196	250	251 (R)	300	304 (R)	55
144	350	197	75	252	500	305	950
145	750	198	450	253	2,000	306	900
146	450	199	775	254	3,000	307	750
147	350	200	400	255	950	308	175
148	2,000	201	20-125	259	600	309 (L)	450
149	300	202	400	260	600	309 (C)	175
150	500	203	325	261	500	309 (R)	450
151	500	204 (L)	50	261	175	310 (L)	125
152	125	204 (R)	150	263	850	310 (R)	95
153	95	204 (F)	25	264	2,000	311 (R)	125
154	650	205 (L)	20	265	200	311 (L)	60
155	150	205 (R)	20	266	400	312	350
156	300	206	150	267	500	313 (L)	375
157 (L)	775	207	100	268	3,000	313 (R)	375
157 (R)	600	208	3,700	269	3,000	314	200
158	300	209	——	270	150	315	300
159	175	210	3,000	271	475	316	350
160	450	211	2,500	272	175	317	400
161	450	212	2,000	274 (L)	100	318	600
162	75	213	3,000	274 (R)	100	319 (L)	50
163	75	214	2,600	275	50	319 (R)	475
164	75	215-227	——	276	150	320	——
165	75	229-231	——	277	200	321	550
166	500	232	650	278	95	322 (L)	300
167	150	233	250	279	150	322 (R)	700
168	300	234	350	280	95	323	750
169	150	235	500	281	40	324	500
170	75	236	60	282 (L)	75	325	100
175	——	237	250-800	282 (R)	300	326	700
176	——	238	90	283	400	327	225
177	——	239	150	285 (L)	400	328	250
178	400	240	475	285 (R)	400	329	650
179	350	241	475	286 (L)	375	330	650
180	450	242 (L)	900	286 (R)	375	331	500
181	275	242 (C)	800	287a	3,000	332	425
182 (L)	200	242 (R)	750	287b	3,000	333	375
182 (R)	350	243	400-900	288	2,800	334	375
183	300	244	400	289	3,000	335	650

Figure	Value ($)	Figure	Value ($)	Figure	Value ($)	Figure	Value ($)
336	650	394	300	444 (C)	275	495 (L)	200
337	650	395	200	444 (R)	200	496	450
338	1200	396	225	445	225	497	200
339	45	397	225	446	250	498 (L)	600
340 (L)	45	398	75-200	447	200-300	498 (R)	1,200
340 (R)	45	399	125	448 (U)	300	499	100-300
341	6	400	600	448 (L)	400	500	50
342	6	401	125	449	175	501	600
343	6	402	100	450	175	502	30-75
344	50	403	135	451	150	503	45
345	175	404	125	452	300	504	60
346	60	405	120	453	150	505	500
347	45	406	100	454	75	506	650
348	55	407	120	455	95	507	90-250
349	55	408	95	456	125	508 (L)	350
350	60	409	90	457	600	508 (C)	350
351	60	410	250	458	700	508 (R)	600
352	60	413	125	459	400	509	175
353	10	414	850	460	700	510	200
354	8	415	600	461	2,500	511	350
355	10	416 (L)	150	462	2,000	512	350
356	15	416 (R)	225	463	150	513	175
357	15	417	850	464 (U)	950	514	175
358	20	418	75	464 (L)	175	515	350
359	10	420 (T)	350	465	150	516	175
360	225	420 (C)	600	466	350	517	250
361 (L)	55	420	75	467	175	518 (L)	100
361 (C)	20	421	350	468	150	518 (R)	125
361 (R)	60	422	400	469	150	519	650
362	20	423	20-50	470	150	520	95
363	20	424	400	471	150	521	175
364	20	425	250	472	150	523	3,000
365	10-35	426	450	473	150	524	3,000
366	5	427	395	474	150	525	3,500
367	10	428	250	475	300	526	3,000
368	75	429	275	476	375	527	1,800
371-373	——	430	265	477	150	528	900
374	375	431 (UL)	600	478	150	529	950
375	300	431 (UR)	600	479	450	530	1,200
376	80	431 (LL)	600	480	400	531	950
377	100	431 (LR)	475	481	275	532	800
378	200-375	432	200	482	400	533	800
379	80-150	433	200	483	300	534	1,200
382	2,000	434	285	484	350	535	1,200
383 (L)	150	435	225	485	750	536 (L)	1,200
383 (R)	150	436	240	486	750	536 (C)	6,000
384	50	437	250	487	700	536 (R)	600
385	600	438	225	488	75	537	950
386	40	439	200	489	125	538	700
387	10-15	440	200	490	75	539	700
388	——	441	250	491	150	540	600
389	375	442	475	492	200	541	850
390	400	443 (U)	225	493	200	542	1,200
391	275	443 (L)	225	494	75	543	600
392	250	444 (L)	200	495 (U)	95	544	450
393	225					545	400

Figure	Value ($)	Figure	Value ($)	Figure	Value ($)
546	600	594 (L)	75	656	400
547	800	594 (C)	150	657	400
548	400	594 (R)	60	658	200
549	400	595	60	659	300
550	1,500	596	50	660	300
551	450	597	25	661	300
552	1,000	598	25	662	200
553	900	599	60	663	225
554	450	600	60		
555	200	601	75		
556	175	602	80		
557	450	603	35		
558	400	604	35		
559	175	605	40		
560	300	606	50		
561	350	607	50		
562 (L)	3,750	608	45		
562 (R)	1,300	609	35		
563	950	610	60		
564 (L)	100	611	65		
564 (R)	400	612	——		
565	450	613	40		
566	300	614	60		
568	300	615	60		
569	250	616	50		
570	225	617	60		
571 (L)	500	618	50		
571 (R)	250	619	40		
572	125	620	35		
573	225	624	2,000		
574	300	628	800		
575	200	629	3,500		
576 (L)	200	630	3,500		
576 (R)	225	631	3,000		
577 (L)	600	632	3,000		
577 (C)	700	633-634	——		
577 (R)	550	635	1,200		
578 (L)	600	636	90		
578 (C)	600	638	250		
578 (R)	300	639	125		
578 (F)	600	640	75		
579	150	641	90		
580	400	642	50		
581	——	643	175		
582	300	644	225		
583	75	645	300		
585	150	647	50		
586	100	648	75		
587	100	649	175		
588	100	650	90		
589	75	651	75		
590	175	652	30-300		
591	125	653	275		
592	75	654	50		
593	100	655	75		